PROBLEM SOLVING WITH YOUNG CHILDREN

Other Redleaf Press Books by Ann Gadzikowski

Young Architects at Play: STEM Activities for Young Children

Robotics for Young Children: STEM Activities and Simple Coding

Creating a Beautiful Mess: Ten Essential Play Experiences for a Joyous Childhood

Challenging Exceptionally Bright Children in Early Childhood Classrooms

Story Dictation: A Guide for Early Childhood Professionals

Problem Solving with Young Children

Building Creativity, Critical Thinking, and Resilience

Ann Gadzikowski

www.redleafpress.org
800-423-8309

Published by Redleaf Press
10 Yorkton Court
St. Paul, MN 55117
www.redleafpress.org

First edition 2022
Cover design by Jesse Hughes
Cover photographs/illustrations by Leonid / pahis / Olesia Bilkei / Halfpoint / fizkes / stock.adobe.com
Interior design by Douglas Schmitz
Typeset in Utopia and Protipo
Printed in the United States of America
29 28 27 26 25 24 23 22 1 2 3 4 5 6 7 8

Library of Congress Cataloging-in-Publication Data

Names: Gadzikowski, Ann, author.
Title: Problem solving with young children : building creativity, critical thinking, and resilience / Ann Gadzikowski.
Description: St. Paul : Redleaf Press, 2022. | Includes bibliographical references and index. | Summary: "Turn everyday frustrations into teachable moments. Young children encounter problems, mistakes, and accidents that challenge them daily. Helping children conquer everyday frustrations fosters the creativity, critical thinking, and resilience that enables children to thrive in a formidable world"-- Provided by publisher.
Identifiers: LCCN 2022012216 (print) | LCCN 2022012217 (ebook) | ISBN 9781605547671 (paperback) | ISBN 9781605547688 (ebook)
Subjects: LCSH: Problem solving--Study and teaching (Early childhood)--Activity programs. | Critical thinking--Study and teaching (Early childhood)--Activity programs. | Creative thinking--Study and teaching (Early childhood)--Activity programs. | Resilience (Personality trait) in children.
Classification: LCC LB1139.35.A37 G338 2022 (print) | LCC LB1139.35.A37 (ebook) | DDC 370.15/24--dc23/eng/20220427
LC record available at https://lccn.loc.gov/2022012216
LC ebook record available at https://lccn.loc.gov/2022012217

Printed on acid-free paper

To new teachers everywhere,
may your journey begin
with joy and grace.

And in grateful recognition of
Mary Pat Martin,
my first mentor.

Contents

Foreword

"Uh-oh!" Blocks crash, a child cries, and a teacher comes running. "I didn't do it! Am I in trouble?" The teacher might be wondering the same thing if a colleague, administrator, or parent is watching this moment of distress and disarray in the classroom. After reading *Problem Solving with Young Children*, we can see that no one is in trouble. On the contrary, we are all in luck.

Ann Gadzikowski has written this guidebook for teachers, caregivers, and school administrators, capturing what an experienced early childhood teacher says when the unexpected happens. This book is both practical and well-grounded in current educational and child development research. Ann captures how teachers think when they are on the same wavelength as the children in their care, becoming the teachers children need in each new moment of surprise, distress, or challenge.

Ann takes us to the place where problems and mistakes are the opposite of trouble, where children and teachers remain open to opportunities for learning that involve thinking, feeling, and strengthening relationships with peers and teachers. The result frees everyone from feeling blamed; it clears the air so problem solving can begin carrying everyone forward into a new place of understanding where things work more smoothly once again. When problems are resolved, children come to trust one another and their teacher more deeply, trusting the process of learning in school.

Ann illustrates how teachers working within a variety of curricular approaches can bring a sensitivity to children's fears and an awareness of the kinds of issues children worry about when questions emerge or uncertainty arises. She reminds us that these are exactly the moments we need for learning to happen, and she helps us remember how to receive and enter these most important and valuable moments of the day. She sets out what teachers think and do in unsettled moments: how to move into the scene, hold each child in safety, and respond to the dilemma at hand with confidence.

The author models the playful, inquisitive way teachers and children connect with one another when children are having a good day in school. The key to the approach she offers is to forgo judging the child or oneself when slipups happen and problems unfold. In these moments, our feelings of annoyance or frustration can strangle our ability to reason well and teach. Instead, Ann invites us to be curious about what just happened, asking what kind of problem has just surfaced, welcoming it, and approaching the moment with a series of questions.

One of the most helpful ways to learn and grow in the craft of teaching is to visit the classrooms of more-experienced teachers to observe and discuss what is unfolding. In today's world, with many strains on a teacher's time, visiting classrooms is not always possible. A strength of Ann's book is the way she draws on the writings of master teacher Vivian Gussin Paley, one of her role models and one of the best we have in educational literature. Mrs. Paley's books attest to the premise that problems are everywhere in a classroom, whether they come cloaked in complaints concerning what's fair, the frequent misunderstandings that emerge in pretend play, challenges when negotiating friendships, or many other forms. Ann discusses a variety of excerpts from Mrs. Paley's work to provide a snapshot of the principles of problem solving at work among young children and their teacher.

This book is written for beginners, and as I read it, I realized that *all* of us are beginners at times. The author explores the scenes of everyday moments of surprise, upset, curiosity, and disappointment that shape every single day for teachers and children: in the classroom, on the playground, and likely at home. The author invites us to approach moments when something breaks or spills, a feeling gets hurt, or materials are lost or misplaced with excitement, knowing that the children and teacher are a few moments away from a breakthrough, a resolution. The author's approach here is so simple that it might seem on first read as if, "Of course! I can do this!" But some days even a veteran teacher finds that the problems come too fast and relentlessly to feel sure about anything. This book prepares the beginner and reminds those with experience how to respond: how to start a conversation that will calm and open the way to resolution with everyone involved, including parents when needed.

The pressures on teachers can sometimes leave us forgetting our best skills momentarily. Having this book in the classroom and on the kitchen table at home can remind novices and more veteran teachers how to step back into our best selves to create the setting and relationships where we thrive and can't wait to come back for more. This book makes clear what we do as professional teachers who bring children together into a powerful community experience of safety, fairness, kindness, and clear reasoning.

Teachers are the emissaries for children's futures. We have the opportunity to provide children with daily problem-solving experiences that will serve them well as they face futures full of serious and complex problems. As Ann writes, "Problems are an unlimited natural resource in your classroom." With this book in hand, teachers can align their teaching with solving problems while simultaneously preparing children to tackle challenges in a collaborative, thoughtful way that will strengthen the society of the future. Teaching young children is rewarding because we step into a place of hope every day. This book reminds us how to find a route forward that holds promise for all children's futures, and how to travel that pathway with them frequently.

—Gillian Dowley McNamee, PhD
Professor, Early Childhood Education
Erikson Institute

Acknowledgments

The day I interviewed for my first preschool teaching job, Chicago had just experienced a torrential rain and severe thunderstorms. Power was out in some areas, and many streets were flooded. I arrived at Evanston Day Nursery (EDN) late in the afternoon. There were still half a dozen children who had not yet been picked up. I observed how the teachers took the children outdoors to see the flooded playground. The children were fascinated by the way the sandbox had transformed from a play area into a small lake. I saw how the teachers listened to their questions and encouraged their interest. One of the teachers helped the children find leaves and sticks to float on the surface of the water. I could see that this school was a place where a negative setback like a summer storm could become inspiration for curiosity and exploration.

I got that teaching job at EDN, and most everything I've done in early childhood education has been shaped by my experience there. I'm grateful to the amazing educators who were my EDN coworkers, including Mary Pat Martin, Teri Talan, Delores Malone, Jim Gillette, and Larissa Mulholland, to name just a few. I'm also grateful to the many educators from other programs who contributed their ideas and examples for this book. Thank you, all, for sharing your wisdom with me.

I also want to thank Redleaf Press and Think Small for supporting my work as an author for more than a decade now. A special thank-you goes to my editor Melissa York for her kindness and expertise.

CHAPTER 1

Looking for the Light in Broken Places

Young children today are growing up in a world with deep and complex problems. Climate change. Natural disasters. Deadly pandemics. Gun violence. Systemic racism and inequality. Even on a good day, the world can seem broken beyond repair. And yet our work as teachers and caregivers for children requires us to find light and joy in the broken places.

But here's the good news. The actual process of solving problems is where we find that light and joy. The profound creativity and resilience of human beings is demonstrated in the ways we have overcome the most difficult challenges. Look at the development of vaccines for COVID-19. In record time, scientists came together and produced not just one but several highly effective vaccines. And what we have learned along the way will help us develop other vaccines and treatments for future diseases.

As educators, we must think of problems as an unlimited natural resource generated inside our own classrooms. Every problem, large or small, is an opportunity to learn and grow.

Embrace Mistakes

For many years, I coordinated summer programs for children at Northwestern University that were affectionately nicknamed "nerd camps." One of our most popular offerings was called Rocket Science, a weeklong class in which seven- and eight-year-olds built and tested their own rocket inventions. We made stomp rockets, balloon rockets, vinegar-and-baking-soda rockets, and more.

Our Rocket Science class ran many times over many summers, yet every time I observed one of the classes, I saw how the children who struggled and tinkered with their rockets were the ones who learned the most. If a child's rocket construction worked the first time, it was usually due to luck, not skill or knowledge. But if a child's rocket didn't work—if it fell over on the launchpad or flew sideways—the child had to tinker and rethink the design, often talking and collaborating with other young scientists who were also struggling. They had to think about balance and symmetry, for example, and adjust the construction of their design to make it fly straight. I noticed how these struggling tinkerers were often the most eager to come to class each morning and try something new, and they were often the most articulate in explaining how their rockets worked. These were also the children who sometimes cried on the last day of class because they didn't want Rocket Science to end.

Simply put, we learn more from our mistakes than from our successes.

Learning requires risk and experimentation. In the field of education, at every level there are specific approaches to teaching and learning that recognize the power of this struggle. You may have heard of problem-based learning or inquiry-based learning, or read about the importance of critical thinking or design thinking. These terms and approaches are usually discussed in relation to the education of older children and young adults.

Yet the comprehensive idea that weaves together all of these approaches—that we are most engaged in learning when we have the opportunity to actively solve interesting problems—is absolutely relevant to early childhood education. Even very young children can be encouraged to play an active role in the problem-solving process. In short, the beauty of active problem solving (as compared to learning by listening to a prepared lesson or memorizing facts) is that most real-world problems have more than one solution. Problem solvers must be creative and think of multiple options and ideas before deciding which solution to try. And solving a problem, like launching a rocket, does not always go well the first time. We must be resilient thinkers who are willing to try and try again, and we must be critical thinkers who can evaluate what went well and what needs to change.

The Curriculum Is Everything That Happens

The word *curriculum* means a course of study, or the ideas and information that we want children to learn. Yet a holistic, inclusive approach to early childhood education acknowledges that the curriculum is really everything that happens in the classroom.

When I think about how teachers facilitate problem solving with young children, I'm reminded of the beloved picture book *If You Give a Mouse a Cookie* by Laura Joffe Numeroff. The story begins:

> If you give a mouse a cookie, he's going to ask for a glass of milk.
> When you give him the milk, he'll probably ask you for a straw.

As the story goes on, each step leads to another step, until we come back again to the cookie. Sometimes the steps make sense, such as needing a straw for drinking, and sometimes the steps are fanciful and silly, such as looking at your face in the mirror to check for a milk mustache. Similarly, if you ask young children to solve a problem, their suggestions will sometimes make sense, but some ideas will be surprisingly quirky and creative.

Here's an example. As a teacher, you may be required to teach a lesson on a specific topic such as shapes. Perhaps you diligently prepare for your lesson the night before by cutting out a paper circle, square, and triangle that you will use as teaching props. But the next day, as you rush to get to work on time, you accidentally leave the paper shapes on your kitchen table. Now it's lesson time, your preschoolers are gathering on the rug, and you suddenly realize you don't have your paper shapes. What do you do?

When you view every problem as a teachable moment and you see your curriculum as inclusive of everything that happens in your classroom, the missing shapes now become an opportunity for collaborative learning and problem solving.

You might say to the children, "Oh no! I have a problem. Today I want to teach you about shapes, but I accidentally left my paper shapes at home." Then you might invite the children to help you solve the problem. "What should we do?"

The children will likely make a variety of suggestions, both practical and whimsical. You could drive home and get the shapes. If that would take too long, you could borrow a helicopter and fly to your house. Or maybe you could make some new shapes. Invariably, the children will offer to help.

Perhaps you will seize the moment, grab some construction paper, and say, "I like these ideas. Let's make a paper circle. Now, tell me about circles so I know what to do." The children may describe a circle as "round" or "like a ball," they may use movement and gestures to show you the shape of a circle, or they may point to examples of circles in the classroom.

In their eagerness to take an active role in the problem solving, the children will be drawn into the learning process in a way that is much more authentic and compelling than simply teaching a lesson about shapes. The lesson may go so well that you'll decide to "forget" your lesson materials again soon.

What a liberating idea, that we can use problems as opportunities for learning. This works especially well in classrooms that already use an emergent curriculum approach. With an emergent curriculum approach, teachers develop their curriculum in response to children's emerging interests and inquiries. The Reggio approach is one example of an emergent curriculum process. Reggio-inspired teachers observe children's interests; provide provocations (experiences or props that spark deeper conversations and explorations); and facilitate the development of projects that engage children in representing their ideas in many ways, such as with drawings, clay sculptures, and paintings, as well as with movement, dramatic play, and music.

Another example of an emergent curriculum process is the project approach, as defined by Lilian Katz and developed by educators such as Judy Harris Helm. In the project approach, the teacher identifies a topic of interest to the children and facilitates the development of a large collaborative project. What all emergent curriculum approaches have in common are that the teachers are responsive to children's interests and that there is a significant amount of collaboration.

When teachers welcome problems as valuable opportunities for learning, every conflict, mistake, and accident in the classroom is a potential inspiration for an emergent curriculum. We'll discuss how to identify and build a curriculum around problem solving throughout this book.

A Special Note to the Brand-New Teacher

A particular tender vulnerability comes with being a new teacher, as you step into your first classroom and meet your first students. Most of us are desperate to do well, and most of us struggle.

I was a first-year teacher for about three years. My first teaching job was a part-time preschool position in a small community-based child care center. I had a college degree but no training specific to early childhood education. Yet I had a wonderful mentor and a supportive team who encouraged me to go back to school and become a credentialed teacher. I taught part-time for three years while I went to graduate school at the Erikson Institute in Chicago.

Just as I was gaining some confidence in teaching preschool, I found myself teaching older children. To earn a state teaching certificate, I had to do my student teaching in a combined first- and second-grade classroom. On one of the days when my graduate school adviser was observing me, I taught a math lesson that involved using a baseball scorecard. I was eager to show my adviser that I had found a creative way to connect math to the children's interest in sports. Yet as I was teaching the lesson, one of the second graders raised his hand and pointed out to me that I was doing it wrong. This child clearly had much more experience with baseball scorekeeping than I did, and he was eager to point out my mistakes. I was so very embarrassed. I'm even blushing now as I write this, years later.

Being a new teacher is hard! I wanted so desperately to show my adviser that I was a good teacher, and in truth I was probably doing fine, but I thought I had to be perfect and I couldn't bear to make mistakes.

This book is dedicated to new teachers because I understand how difficult it can be to begin this important work. I wish I had known that problems and mistakes are such valuable resources. I wish I had given myself permission to make mistakes. I wish I had understood that when teachers approach mistakes with grace and curiosity, we are giving the children a gift. We are showing them how to find the light and joy in this dark world.

To new teachers, I say:

- Accept that you will make mistakes.
- Expect and welcome problems.
- Learn from other teachers. Watch what they do when they make a mistake. Watch how they respond when a child makes a mistake.
- Be patient and allow time for learning and reflection.

As teachers of young children, it is our responsibility to raise a new generation of problem solvers. We begin doing this by modeling how to make mistakes with grace and curiosity.

Research Supports Problem Solving

Reading and math are usually considered the most important subjects taught in early childhood and the primary grades. Educators and families see these two academic areas as foundational for school success, and for good reason. At the same time, there is a growing body of research finding that problem solving is an essential foundational academic skill. Much of this research connects the dots between children's participation in active problem solving and children's later success in school and beyond.

GRIT AND GROWTH MINDSET

We can't talk about problem solving with children without acknowledging two popular ideas in education—psychologist Angela Duckworth's concept of grit and Stanford professor Carol Dweck's concept of a growth mindset. I believe that one of these ideas is useful to early childhood educators and one is not.

In her best-selling book *Grit: The Power of Passion and Perseverance*, Duckworth (2016) asserts that the key to academic and life success is a thing called "grit," which she defines as a passion for and perseverance toward long-term goals. Many fans of Duckworth's work promote the idea that grit is something teachers and families must intentionally nurture in children so that they learn to set goals and stick with them, even when they encounter problems and mistakes along the way.

But the concept of grit as defined by Duckworth doesn't align well with a developmental view of early childhood in which young children naturally explore a wide range of topics and ideas through open-ended activities such as play. Young children are rarely capable of creating long-term goals. It's true that some young children demonstrate exceptional talent for activities like gymnastics or violin playing, and adults may help shape and encourage these gifts in ways that lead to long-term success. But these children are the exception and not the rule. That type of intense, goal-directed problem solving is not what we will explore in this book.

I would argue, however, that Dweck's concept of a growth mindset is indeed relevant to how we think about and facilitate problem solving in early childhood classrooms. Dweck's research suggests that children with a growth mindset see themselves as flexible, capable learners, while those with a fixed mindset believe that being smart is a predetermined thing. When children believe they can get smarter, they are willing to put effort into learning and they can recover from their mistakes. New research in neuroscience supports Dweck's assertion that our beliefs about ourselves as learners shape our brains (Owens and Tanner 2017).

One element of Dweck's work on growth mindsets that is particularly interesting to me is her research on girls and math, which shows that girls are more likely than boys to give up when faced with difficult math problems (Dweck 2007). Dweck suggests that girls tend to see math ability as a gift, something you are born with, while boys tend to see math as a set of skills and concepts that you learn over time. Because of this research, helping children develop a growth mindset becomes an important opportunity to advocate for equity in our classrooms.

While Dweck's research was conducted with older children, it suggests to me that early childhood educators can help support all children of all identities by nurturing the development of growth mindsets. The strategies and techniques described in this book—with an emphasis on experimentation, learning from mistakes, and trying out multiple solutions—are well aligned with those that support a growth mindset.

STRENGTH-BASED CARE AND TEACHING

Also inherently relevant to problem solving is the idea that children benefit when teachers and caregivers focus on their strengths rather than weaknesses. Strength-based care and teaching is also sometimes called "asset-informed care and teaching." Many conversations about strengths and assets among early childhood professionals are in response to new research and literature about the impact of trauma on young children and families.

In her book *The Deepest Well: Healing the Long-Term Effects of Childhood Adversity*, Nadine Burke Harris (2018), a pediatrician and the surgeon general of California, describes how childhood trauma such as abuse, illness, poverty, and systemic racism can have profound and lifelong health effects. Our growing understanding of the impact of adverse childhood experiences (ACEs) helps early childhood professionals appreciate that sometimes children's challenging behaviors and difficulties with learning can be better understood in the context of trauma.

At the same time, experts such as Ellen Galinsky of Families and Work Institute remind us that if we look at vulnerable children only through the lens of trauma, there is a risk that we will see only what is broken and miss children's strengths and talents. Galinksy (2019) writes that we must expand "beyond these problem-focused, trauma-laced concepts to narratives and solutions that are rooted in children's and families' assets. . . . Successful interventions are asset-based, focusing and expanding on what children and adults are already doing that's right."

A problem-solving approach that lifts up children's curiosity, questions, and ideas aligns well with Galinsky's concept of asset-informed care. A collaborative and creative approach to problem solving in the classroom helps counter the impact of trauma by nurturing resilience in young children.

WHAT IS RESILIENCE?

Resilience is the ability to adapt to difficult situations. We can all agree that resilience is a good thing for children to develop, but how exactly does that happen?

Educators and researchers including Paul Tough (2012), author of *How Children Succeed: Grit, Curiosity, and the Hidden Power of Character*, assert that resilience can't be taught through traditional teaching methods. There is no resilience curriculum or lesson plan. The development of resilience begins in early childhood and is shaped by the interactions between children and adults—families, teachers, and other caregivers.

Tough's research suggests that if adults respond to children's strong emotions harshly or unpredictably, children are less likely to develop the ability to respond to challenges. But if adults respond to children's emotions in a sensitive and measured way, they are more likely to develop the capacity to cope.

This emerging research on resilience emphasizes the importance of social and emotional learning in early childhood classrooms. When teachers learn to respond to children's mistakes, problems, and conflicts with sensitivity, encouragement, and a growth mindset, children have a better chance of developing the resilience that will allow them to succeed in school, in the workplace, and in social relationships.

How to Use This Book

Each chapter of this book explains how early childhood teachers, providers, and families can take the problems, mistakes, and accidents that occur in the daily lives of young children and turn them into teachable moments.

We'll also shine a light on what children learn along the way: the social skills, emotional intelligence, language and communication skills, and STEM (science, technology, engineering, and math) skills that children grow as they participate in an authentic, meaningful problem-solving process.

Each chapter stands alone as a single topic. You are welcome to read the chapters in order or jump ahead to the topics that interest you most. This chapter serves as an introduction and overview.

Chapter 2 provides background information about how children think and learn and why experimentation, trial and error, conversation, and hands-on experiences are so important. This chapter also presents the framework and goals for an antibias approach and explains how children's developing understandings of self, identity, and differences play an important role in how we navigate a problem-solving process.

Chapter 3 focuses on the art of teaching. This chapter examines how making mistakes makes us better teachers and caregivers and how letting go of rigid expectations—of ourselves as well as the children—frees us to embrace problems and mistakes as rich opportunities for learning. In chapter 3, we'll also look at the work of a master teacher, Vivian Gussin Paley, and discuss what we can learn from it about how to solve problems with children.

Chapter 4 is a primer on asking great questions and, more important, really listening to children's responses. This chapter is a tool kit of conversation starters, questions, and prompts that teachers can always keep at the ready.

Chapter 5 examines common problems that happen during the daily routines of an early childhood classroom, such as during snacks, naps, and transitions. The chapter includes examples of problem-solving scenarios (like not having enough spoons for the applesauce at the snack table) and strategies and techniques for facilitating problem solving in the moment.

Chapter 6 focuses on social relationships and social conflicts. This chapter explores the problems that frequently arise between young children as they learn to get along and make friends, such as conflicts around sharing toys or negotiating who gets to play with whom.

Chapter 7 looks closely at issues of communication and examines the role of language when children are experiencing and solving problems. The chapter offers strategies to help us listen, observe, respond, and connect with children who have difficulty expressing their feelings and ideas because of developmentally appropriate challenges or because they have language delays or other issues that require facilitation and support.

Chapter 8 explores play and focuses on the kinds of STEM learning that arise naturally when children have the opportunity to work out creative problems during play. This chapter provides strategies for supporting STEM learning through experimentation, design thinking, and the scientific method.

Chapter 9 provides tools, tips, and ideas for using problems and the problem-solving process to build a curriculum and to demonstrate learning and growth. This chapter includes ideas for documenting the problem-solving process for use in curriculum planning and assessment practices as well as strategies for using everyday teachable moments to meet curriculum standards and fulfill assessment requirements.

In chapter 10, we conclude with a celebration of problems, mistakes, accidents, and uncomfortable surprises. We'll discuss how to include parents and family members in the problem-solving process at school. This chapter offers strategies and suggestions for working with families to help them understand the value of problems and for coaching parents on how to use many of the strategies presented in the book.

Each chapter also includes quotes, anecdotes, and advice from a diverse mix of teachers, providers, and children who have found their own ways to bring light and joy to the problem-solving process.

> I make mistakes all the time! I show the children that everybody makes mistakes. I learned this from being around amazing teachers and observing them. I saw in my own child what happens when

they're afraid to answer a teacher's question. This is their first schooling ever. We can't let them lose the joy. We want them to love school.

—S.G., pre-K teacher in Chicago, Illinois

CHAPTER 2

Thinking and Learning

Scientists studying the human brain have made remarkable discoveries about the kinds of experiences that support healthy neurodevelopment in young children. According to the Center on the Developing Child at Harvard University (2007), the first years of life are a time of incredible growth within the brain, with more than a million new neural connections formed every second.

During the preschool years, rapid brain growth continues as children develop higher cognitive functions. Early childhood experiences are so important because the brain is still growing and flexible early in life. What happens in a child's brain during the first five years sets the stage for lifelong learning.

Among the most important experiences that feed children's brains are their interactions with other people. In particular, serve-and-return interactions shape the brain. These are interactions in which a caregiver, such as a parent or teacher, responds to a child's cues by offering encouraging words or actions that bring out additional engagement from the child—exactly the kinds of exchanges that happen when adults facilitate a problem-solving experience with children. A child pulls a toy from the shelf, but it slips from her hand and falls on the floor. She looks at the face of her caregiver, as if to say, "Am I in trouble?" The caregiver smiles and says, "Uh-oh! The toy fell down. What should we do?" The child's *serve* in this type of interaction can be a problem or mistake. The adult can extend and deepen the interaction by providing a supportive *return* that invites the child to engage and take an active role in solving a problem.

Moreover, mistakes are good for the brain. Neuroscience researchers have shown that making mistakes sets off productive brain activity. Carol Dweck, the psychologist who developed the concept of a growth mindset, has said that "every time a student makes a mistake . . . they grow a synapse" (Boaler 2016, 11). A synapse is the space through which an electrical signal moves between parts of the brain when learning takes place. Psychologist Jason Moser and collaborators found that when people make mistakes, there is increased electrical activity in their brains. This activity may be caused by the conflict between a correct response and a mistake. Moser concluded that our conscious attention to mistakes causes additional enriching brain activity (Moser et al. 2011).

Let's acknowledge what we already know, intuitively and from experience, about the value of wrestling with a tricky challenge. Surely many untrained caregivers like grannies and nannies have always known intuitively how to pose problems to the children in their care—problems that promote learning and exploration. In families, we sometimes call this "learning the hard way" or "the school of hard knocks." Even educator Friedrich Froebel, heralded as the "father of kindergarten," looked to the caregivers and tradespeople in his nineteenth-century German community as models and used their work for his learning occupations such as weaving and sewing. Froebel recognized that practical tasks and challenges like threading a cord through a bead or weaving a strip of paper present valuable learning opportunities for children.

Of course, the most valuable learning opportunity of all is play.

Learning through Play

If you have spent any amount of time playing with young children or observing their play, you probably already know the importance of play in learning. To learn usually requires some level of risk and active experimentation, with the opportunity to try something one way and then try it again another way. Putting together a puzzle, for example, often requires trying different puzzle pieces, rotating each puzzle piece first one way and then another until it falls into place.

Discovering how children learn and how they construct their understanding of the world was the life's work of Swiss epistemologist Jean Piaget. According to Piaget, preschool children are in a "preoperational stage" of cognitive development, which means they are just beginning to learn to think with abstraction and apply logic. Children at this age require direct experience with physical objects like blocks, balls, and puzzles to try out their ideas and make meaning.

I'm particularly fascinated by the fact that Piaget created his developmental framework by studying his own children, Jacqueline, Laurent, and Lucienne. Most academic researchers frown upon studying family members, questioning our ability to maintain accuracy and objectivity when working with the people we love. Yet I'm charmed by the idea of Piaget the parent observing and reflecting on, with profound insight and creativity, the play experiences of his own children. By being willing and eager to sit on the floor with his toddlers and pay attention to how they manipulated objects as they played, Piaget convinced the world that children thrive when they do the work of learning themselves.

> A problem means that you've done something wrong. I try to do stuff, but something goes wrong. Like I tried to build Legos, and a Lego piece got lost. I tried to look for it. It took me nine hours to find it.
>
> —Beau, five years old

While much of Piaget's work focuses on how children engage with physical objects, the work of Russian child psychologist Lev Vygotsky expands our understanding of how children learn in the context of relationships and through social interactions. Vygotsky's research demonstrates how children learn from one another every day, emphasizing the role of social interactions in learning.

I think of Vygotsky when I observe young children in a preschool classroom working together to solve a problem that arises during pretend play, especially when they come up with a solution on their own, without the help of a teacher. Suppose, for example, two preschool children are pretending to be a mommy and a baby.

The pretend baby has crawled under a blanket and cries, "Waa! Waa! I'm taking a nap."

Another child joins them and wants to be a baby too.

The other two insist there can be only one baby.

"There can be two babies," argues the third. "We can have twin babies."

"No, no twins. Just one sad baby," insists the child cuddled under the blanket. "There's only room for one in the bed."

The pretend mommy suggests, "You can be an older baby who's awake."

"Okay," agrees the third child.

This is the kind of negotiated problem solving that can happen only when children play together freely and independently. They are coming up with ideas together that they wouldn't encounter alone. Vygotsky's theory of social constructivism suggests that children's cognitive development is sparked by these exchanges and that these experiences help children become more resourceful when future problems arise.

The Process of Problem Solving

The research of both Piaget and Vygotsky emphasizes the importance of hands-on real-world experience, demonstrating in action why experimentation, trial and error, conversation, and collaboration are such important experiences. Their work informs how we understand and facilitate the problem-solving process with young children.

Curriculum programs that focus on teaching problem solving are often targeted to serve older children in elementary grades, middle school, and high school. *Problem-based learning* and *inquiry-based learning* are two terms frequently used to describe a teacher-facilitated approach to teaching independent learning and thinking skills. For example, at the University of Illinois Center for Innovation in Teaching and Learning, a teaching method for problem-based learning (PBL) uses complex real-world problems as the vehicle to promote student learning. This approach is valued as an alternative to direct instruction of facts and concepts.

There are some important takeaways from these kinds of PBL programs that are relevant and developmentally appropriate for our work with young children. Of prime relevance is the concept that problem solving is a *process*, not a single moment or an isolated action. John Dewey, a progressive American educator, can be credited with shining a light on the value of problem solving as a learning process. Dewey's work was a significant influence on the development of many of the inquiry-based learning and problem-based curriculum approaches used today at all grade levels.

In his landmark book *How We Think*, Dewey (1910) suggests that problem solving in the classroom can be a five-phase process.

Phase 1: A Felt Difficulty or Indeterminate Situation

This is the time when the problem arises. The teacher may present a problem, but ideally the student observes and discovers a problem on their own. For example, in the Rocket Science class mentioned in the previous chapter, a frequent problem was a rocket failing to launch.

Phase 2: Locating and Defining the Problem

This is the point in the process when we focus on what has gone wrong. Perhaps we notice a crack or gap in the side of our rocket. We might define the problem as a leak in the chamber holding the fuel for the vinegar-and-baking-soda rocket.

Phase 3: A Suggested Solution

We must now think of a way to fix the problem. Vygotsky's work suggests this step is best accomplished in collaboration with others, perhaps with an older child who has had some additional experience building rockets. We might decide to use tape to patch the gap in the rocket.

Phase 4: Refining the Suggestion

Dewey's problem-solving process includes this step in which there is a deeper examination of the suggested solution. This step may or may not happen among young children. As we know from Piaget, children are hands-on learners and may jump ahead to phase 5.

Phase 5: Testing the Suggestion
The final step of inquiry for Dewey is testing the suggested solution and observing the results.

Dewey's suggested framework for problem solving was published more than a hundred years ago, yet his work influences today's PBL approaches. The process is more important than the product. Learning happens along the route, not at the destination.

Inquiry and Design Thinking

Other problem-solving approaches that emphasize process are inquiry-based learning and design thinking. Inquiry-based learning is similar to PBL except that the process is driven by a question rather than a problem. Design thinking, a concept that originated in business rather than education, is an approach to solving problems that embraces mistakes and encourages multiple iterations, or solutions. Design thinking, also known as "design engineering," has made its way into early childhood education. This is in part, I believe, because design engineering is the most similar to play of all the approaches to problem solving found in the broader field of education. The process of design engineering (described in the following text) might remind you of Dewey's framework from 1910, but it became popular among computer programmers and educators who teach coding.

Question
The process begins with a question. Suppose a pair of preschoolers has noticed that the wooden dollhouse in their classroom has no staircase. A child might ask, "How can the little dollhouse people get upstairs?"

Imagine
The next step in the design engineering process involves imagining different ways to answer the question or solve the problem. The children might

brainstorm several ideas about how the dolls can get upstairs, such as by building a set of stairs for the dollhouse, adding an elevator, using a ladder, or simply pretending that they are going up an imaginary set of stairs.

Plan

Next, the design engineers make a plan for their first iteration or solution. Suppose the children decide to build a set of stairs. They must plan for what materials they will use, such as blocks, and where they will position the stairs. The planning phase may take just a few minutes or, when solving more complex problems, several days.

Create

This is the most active step in the design engineering process: implementing the plan and creating a solution, or at least attempting to solve the problem for the first time. Here the children may construct a staircase next to the dollhouse using wooden blocks.

Improve

Now it's time to test the solution. How did it work? Suppose the block staircase topples the first time the children try walking the dolls upstairs. Rather than giving up and moving on, the design engineering process challenges us to innovate for continual improvement by creating multiple iterations. Now we've come full circle, because the next step is asking another question: "How can we make the stairs stronger?" And the process begins again.

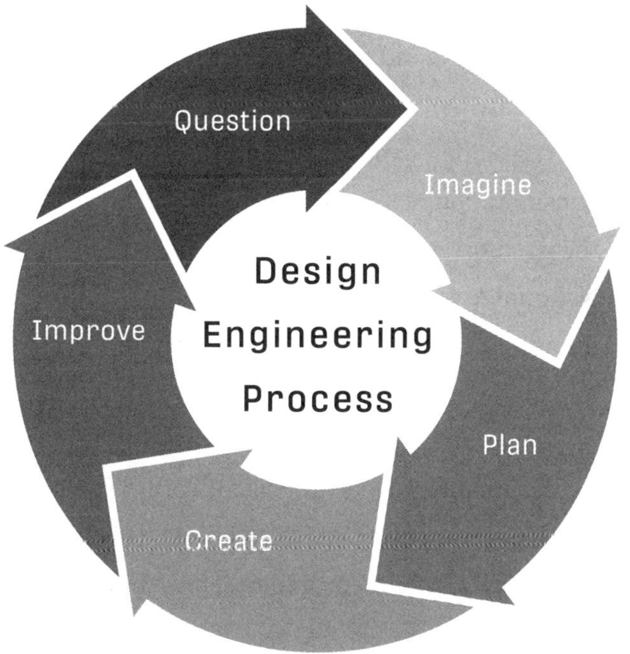

The beauty of design engineering is that failure is baked into the process. It is a cyclical process that leads back to the beginning. The steps in a design engineering process are usually represented as a circle rather than a straight line.

Free play, like design engineering, is cyclical. Children frequently loop back again and again to the play scenarios they find most fascinating and satisfying (such as pretending to be superheroes), tweaking and adjusting as they learn more and more. Play also frequently involves mistakes and failure: the block structure falls down, a puzzle piece is missing, a friend pretends to be a lion instead of a unicorn.

Early childhood educators can use the design engineering process intentionally to develop an emergent problem-solving experience. In their article "Growing in STEM. The Design Process: Engineering Practices in Preschool," early childhood educators Jolyn Blank and Stefanie Lynch (2018) describe how an ordinary day in the sandbox sparked the question "How can we transport water from the porch to the sandbox?" This led to a teacher-facilitated design engineering process that included the five steps: question, imagine, plan, create, and improve. This process will be examined further in chapter 8.

Context, Identity, and Antibias Goals

Each problem and every approach to that problem happen in a unique context: a time and a place involving people—children, teachers, families—with their own identities, experiences, and cultures. The significance of *context* as a core consideration in teaching young children is emphasized in the 2020 revision of the position statement on developmentally appropriate practice (DAP) from the National Association for the Education of Young Children (NAEYC). The Developmentally Appropriate Practice Position Statement is a framework of principles and guidelines to support a teacher's intentional decision-making for practice.

Regarding the importance of context, the position statement states that "all development and learning occur within specific social, cultural, linguistic, and historical contexts" (NAEYC 2020, 6). This is certainly true when young children work at solving problems. How children approach a problem, how they understand the problem, how they collaborate with others, and how they seek solutions will always be influenced by their personal cultural contexts and their identities. Children approach problem solving based on how they know the world, reflecting their family's traditions, values, and experiences. Teachers must consider how children's developing understandings of self, identity, and differences play into their problem-solving process.

As we learned from Vygotsky, in early childhood classrooms, learning happens in relationships—the relationships between teachers and children, as well as the relationships among the children who play and learn together. As educators, we are best equipped to support and facilitate learning and problem solving when we establish trusting relationships with children and when we are open to seeing each child as a unique individual. Remember, we are role models for children, demonstrating how to listen and respect one another, even when problems arise.

Some of the best tools for helping educators engage in responsive relationships and interactions can be found in antibias education. According to the seminal work led by Louise Derman-Sparks, there are four interrelated goals of antibias education, which are relevant to both children and adults:

Goal 1: Identity: "Children will demonstrate self-awareness, confidence, family pride, and positive social identities."

Goal 2: Diversity: "Children will express comfort and joy with human diversity; use accurate language for human differences; and form deep, caring connections across all dimensions of human diversity."

Goal 3: Justice: "Children will increasingly recognize unfairness (injustice), have language to describe unfairness, and understand that unfairness hurts."

Goal 4: Action: "Children will demonstrate a sense of empowerment and the skills to act, with others or alone, against prejudice and/or discriminatory action."
(Derman-Sparks and Edwards 2020, 5)

These four antibias goals are essential tools for teaching and can be applied more specifically to facilitating a problem-solving process with children. The goals provide a framework for the educator to progress to clearer understandings of both the context for children's learning as well as for educators to directly address the role of bias in actual problems.

Suppose a problem arises at the lunch table. There are six children and only five forks. This becomes a convenient opportunity to pose a math question to the children: "How many forks do we need so everyone can eat?" The question incorporates concepts of counting, addition, and one-to-one correspondence. But suppose that one child insists that we already have enough forks. Is that child wrong? Let's consider the context. Suppose the child's family does not use forks at home. Perhaps the child's cultural practices include using other kinds of utensils or no utensils at all. This context is relevant to how the teacher facilitates the problem-solving process. In this case, the teacher may respond by asking, "Hmm. What are some other ways of eating besides using a fork?"

Acknowledging the child's perspective and experience as well as the family's cultural practices aligns with the first antibias goal for this child by supporting their confidence and family pride. The conversation and problem-solving process also align with the second antibias goal for all children in the group by supporting their comfort with differences. This is what we mean when we talk about "mirrors and windows" in antibias teaching. The teacher's approach affirms and mirrors the child's culture while providing a window into another way of thinking and acting for children who are from a different culture.

As we will discuss later in this book, some problems are caused by bias or directly related to bias, such as when a child refuses to share their toy because "boys can't play with dolls." The third and fourth antibias goals provide a framework for supporting a problem-solving process with this type of conflict. For example, a teacher might facilitate a conversation about fairness by asking open-ended questions about both dolls and gender, such as "What's fun about playing with dolls?" or "What would happen if a boy played with a doll?" Then the teacher might invite the children to come up with ideas for activities that will encourage everyone, not just girls, to play with dolls, such as having a special snack day when children may bring a doll to the snack table. These kinds of conversations and activities can help children recognize unfairness as well as participate in actions that seek to remedy the problem.

We also need tools for recognizing and understanding our own context and our own biases. As the Developmentally Appropriate Practice Position Statement asserts, "Educators must be aware of, and counter, their own and larger societal biases that may undermine a child's positive development and well-being" (NAEYC 2020, 7). For example, we can seek out books and media that challenge our assumptions and deepen our thinking, such as the NAEYC publication *Each and Every Child: Teaching Preschool with an Equity Lens* (Friedman and Mwenelupembe 2020). And we can engage in conversations and relationships with colleagues and friends that expand our circle of understanding. The position statement on DAP goes on to state that "early childhood educators have a professional responsibility to be life-long learners who are able to foster life-long learning in children; in this, they must keep abreast of research developments, while also learning continuously from families and communities they serve" (NAEYC 2020, 7).

Being open to continuous growth and learning is an essential part of teaching. Educators Margie Carter and Deb Curtis, authors of many wonderful books for teachers, suggest that being an effective teacher may be more about nurturing dispositions than building skills. In their book *Training Teachers: A Harvest of Theory and Practice*, Carter and Curtis (1994, 73–77) name "expect continuous change and challenge" and "be willing to take risks and make mistakes" as two of the core dispositions essential for reflective teaching. Whether we are brand-new teachers or long-term veterans of the classroom, welcoming mistakes and entering into a problem-solving process require courage and vulnerability. We must step into the classroom every day with open minds and open hearts.

CHAPTER 3

The Brave Teacher

Every teacher is a new teacher. No matter how many years we've been teaching, there are always new situations and new challenges. In early childhood especially, children grow and develop new skills, abilities, interests, and curiosities at a rapid pace, which means that the classroom dynamics are constantly changing and evolving. Every teacher is a new teacher because every classroom is a living ecosystem. Each step forward in learning presents new challenges.

These challenges—the accidents, conflicts, and mistakes that are an inevitable part of daily life in an early childhood classroom—are opportunities for growth, connection, and problem solving. Turning these lemons into lemonade starts with teachers who have the courage to welcome problems and to serve as role models in the problem-solving process.

Several years ago, I was challenged to summon the courage to make mistakes when I visited Anchorage, Alaska, to teach in a summer robotics program. Even though I had developed robotics programs for children for many years and had published several books on robotics, I felt like a beginning teacher when I stepped into a new classroom in a new school filled with new children from a community and a part of the world that was completely unfamiliar to me.

The challenges I initially encountered were pretty common and unsurprising, including classroom management issues that came up as I got to know the daily schedule and physical environment of the school and adapted my plans and pacing to the needs and interests of the children. What struck me most was that "new teacher" sense of vulnerability and my fear of making mistakes. It had been a long time since I'd had that feeling, and yet even after more than twenty-five years in the field, it was still a challenge to summon the courage and energy to adapt to a new situation.

Another lesson I learned was a deeper understanding of the importance of context in teaching. By *context* I mean the specific social, cultural, linguistic, and historical contexts of the learning community. (As mentioned in the previous chapter, the importance of context is emphasized in NAEYC's position statement on DAP.) Here I was, a white teacher from midwestern Chicago, visiting a school that serves a diverse population of families in Alaska, near the northwest extremity of the Pacific coastline. Although Anchorage is a big city by Alaskan standards, I quickly discovered that living anywhere in Alaska inspires a profound respect for the natural environment. Many children in my class were from families with ties to Alaskan Native culture or with relatives whose work involved protecting Alaskan natural resources.

The importance of this context was highlighted in a spontaneous and unexpected problem-solving experience in my classroom. On the second day of class, as I was still learning basic information about the school and the children, I was working with a small group of children who were building Lego robots on the floor of the classroom. Suddenly I noticed a spider crawling across the floor. My initial response was protective, since I didn't want the spider to scare the children, so I tried, unsuccessfully, to step on the spider without the children noticing. I missed, clumsily, and several children saw what I was doing and immediately spoke up and insisted that I should not kill the spider.

What happened next was a brief but incredible problem-solving experience in which the children took the lead in finding a container to capture the spider, figuring out how to open a window, and successfully releasing the spider outdoors. I did little to facilitate beyond allowing the children to abandon their robots to work on saving the spider. It was a humbling experience, and after time and reflection, it became a key milestone in my understanding and appreciation of mistakes and surprises as valuable problem-solving opportunities.

Showing Our Courage

The problems that require courage from teachers are those, like my Alaskan spider situation, that make us feel the most vulnerable. When we, as teachers, feel like we're supposed to know something or do something right and we are struggling, it's hard to let go of our desire to do well and avoid mistakes. It's hard to abandon our role as the skilled expert.

Classroom management is a challenge for every teacher. Managing transitions from one activity to another, making sure classroom materials are prepared and distributed, expressing and reinforcing clear expectations, and guiding children's behavior are constant challenges in any early childhood setting. Even teachers who are masters of classroom management techniques will inevitably encounter surprises—an unannounced fire drill, a child who doesn't feel well, a spider crawling across the floor.

Another challenge that requires courage comes when we must incorporate new kinds of technology in our teaching. We might be asked to download an app on our phones to take attendance, add a smart speaker to our classroom, or use new software to create digital portfolios. These challenges require courage and perseverance from any educator, especially for those who are not particularly tech-savvy.

It's hard to accept that things will always go wrong. And yet what if, instead of dreading the moment when things fall apart, we welcome the opportunity to solve problems together? That requires courage.

Having the courage to welcome mistakes and problems makes us better teachers, parents, and caregivers. We are role models, and the children learn from our example. If we can show children how to accept surprises, accidents, conflicts, and mistakes with grace and teach them to solve problems by our example, they will be better prepared to learn and succeed in the future, at school as well as in their professional and personal lives. This is the beauty of the growth mindset discussed in chapter 1. When we see ourselves as learners who are growing, the children are more likely to pick up on that mindset and develop their own flexible mindsets as they approach their own problems and challenges.

How do we let go of our fear of mistakes? One teacher I interviewed for this book said, "It's a matter of trust. I know we will get to where we need to be. It's not my agenda. The children help me gain that trust in myself. They have shown me how not to be afraid of the unknown. Trust the child." This comment impressed me because it reveals how serving as a role model goes both ways. We are role models for the children, and in many ways, we learn from the children too. That was certainly my experience when my students insisted we protect the life of the spider in our classroom.

The Mistake-Friendly Classroom

As teachers, preparing ourselves to welcome mistakes and learn from the problem-solving process requires an intentional decision to create a mistake-friendly classroom. Teachers can set the stage for problem solving at the beginning of the school year in the ways we talk about our community.

> I begin the school year by setting an atmosphere and value of being in a caring community. We give care to each other. I intentionally use these words: "How can we give care?" "We are a caring community," and "We can solve this problem."
>
> —M.D., early childhood educator in Chicago, Illinois

Setting the tone for a mistake-friendly classroom must include parents and family members too. As another preschool teacher told me, "Parents can be nervous about their child's success at school. They are expecting their child to learn ABCs and 123s. But I set the tone right away at the beginning of the school year. I say, 'This is going to be a conflict-rich classroom.' The children will learn how to navigate in a mistake-friendly space. We will teach the skills they need to know."

At circle time or in classroom meetings, teachers can show the children their commitment to welcoming problems by role-playing or intentionally making a mistake. A pair of coteachers I know will intentionally call each other by the wrong names to demonstrate to the children how to handle errors and problems: "Oops, I called Ms. Kelly the wrong name. I'm so sorry, Ms. Kelly. I made a mistake." This is an opportunity to show kindness and grace to each other. "Everyone makes mistakes. It's okay to make mistakes here," Ms. Kelly might reply.

Create a list of go-to phrases and statements that teachers, children, and families can use to encourage one another to welcome mistakes, care for one another, and solve problems. These might include the following phrases and statements:

- Everyone makes mistakes.
- We learn from our mistakes.
- Our brains are growing all the time.
- We are problem solvers.
- The more we try, the more we learn.
- Let's figure it out!

Post the list on the wall of your classroom and refer to it often. Add a sign to your door that says, "Mistakes are welcome here!"

Lessons from Vivian Paley

When I talk with teachers I admire who are great at facilitating problem solving in their classrooms, I ask, "How did you learn to do this?" Usually they tell me they learned from other teachers who served as role models. They learned from colleagues, coteachers, and advisers who modeled open and engaging interactions with children around problem solving and conflict resolution.

One of my own role models was Vivian Gussin Paley, who taught preschool and kindergarten at the University of Chicago Laboratory Schools from the 1970s through the 1990s. She authored many award-winning books about storytelling, play, and the social and emotional development of young children, including *Bad Guys Don't Have Birthdays: Fantasy Play at Four, The Boy Who Would Be a*

Helicopter: The Uses of Storytelling in the Classroom, and *You Can't Say You Can't Play*. In 1989 Paley received a MacArthur "genius" grant in recognition of her work.

My favorite Vivian Paley book is *Wally's Stories: Conversations in the Kindergarten* (1981), and my favorite section is called "Pulley" (95–101). In this section, Paley describes how she facilitated a problem-solving process over the course of several weeks. It begins with the delivery of sand for the sensory table.

> When we returned from winter vacation, there was a seventy-five pound bag of sand on the floor in the middle of our circle. The bag was inside of a basket, and I could not move it without scratching the floor.
>
> "Look where Mr. Prentise left our new sand," I said. "How are we going to move it over there by the wall?"

Interestingly, Paley published *Wally's Stories* in 1981, long before STEM was a trending priority in education. Yet the story she tells about how the children solved the problem of the heavy sand aligns well with what's come to be known as "design thinking" and a "design engineering process." As described previously in chapter 2, a design engineering process follows these steps:

- Question
- Imagine
- Plan
- Create
- Improve

In Paley's classroom, the presence of the heavy bag of sand is the spark that inspires the initial **question**: "How are we going to move it over there by the wall?"

The conversation that follows aligns with the next step in the process, **imagine**. Paley documents the children's ideas. Some ideas seem fanciful, such as a child's idea that Superman can come and lift the bag for them. Other children have more practical ideas, like the child who says, "Do it with a rope."

The children make a **plan** to tie the one end of the rope to the basket and the other end of the rope to a child's arm. A child named Lisa volunteers by saying, "I can do it easy if you tie a rope to my arm."

The next step in the design engineering process is **create**, meaning to create the solution that has been planned. Here, Lisa attempts to lift the sand with the rope, but she is unsuccessful. "This is hard," she says. "The rope is too heavy."

Improve is the next step in a design engineering process, and here, also, Paley invites a similar process in her classroom. After Lisa states that "the rope is too heavy," another child suggests that they "use a string." This plan also proves to be unsuccessful. What has happened here in Paley's classroom is what a design engineer might call an "iterative" approach. The word *iterative* means to repeat, and an iterative process is a practice in which an individual or team experiments with creating many solutions to a problem, each seeking to refine and improve the result.

Paley's facilitation of this process is minimal and patient. She allows the children to think, talk, and even struggle at their own pace. She occasionally asks a question. For example, when the string snaps, Wally (the child featured in the title of the book) says, "I knew that would happen."

Paley asks Wally, "How did you know?"

Wally replies, "Real workers never use string."

When the children have exhausted their initial ideas, Paley coaches them gently, stating, "Then we must think of another way."

Paley observes how the children's movements—the swinging of their arms up and down—suggest the action of a pulley. As you may know, a pulley is a wheel that carries a rope or cord on its rim and is one of the fundamental simple machines. A rotating pulley can transmit energy and motion, which is another way of saying that it can be used to lift heavy objects.

Paley, interestingly, resists suggesting a pulley or teaching children about pulleys. She patiently allows the children the opportunity to invent a pulley themselves.

Wally suggests, "Take a big crane and hook it up there on the ceiling and let the crane take it over to that side."

Paley asks, "How would we get the crane into the room?"

Wally replies, "Okay, just hook the crane to the ceiling—not the whole crane."

This leads to a suggestion from a child named Eddie, who says, "No, look. Tie the rope onto a wheel and if we turn the wheel it would go that way, to the other part of the room."

What happens next demonstrates Paley's genius as a teacher. Rather than showing the children a book about pulleys (which is what I probably would have done) and instead of taking the lead and teaching the children how to make a pulley, she does something that not only builds the children's knowledge but also builds their sense of community. Rather than referring them to a book, she refers them to a person, the science teacher at their school. What a fantastic problem-solving strategy—seeking advice and collaboration from someone who might have valuable knowledge or experience.

The big reveal occurs in the high school science classroom. Paley brings the class there, and the teacher tells them, "You've invented a very useful machine. We call it a pulley."

Paley could have ended her story there and called it a great success. But she then describes several attempts she made to inspire the children to apply their understanding of pulleys to other similar problems. She was a bit surprised to see that they did not. When she presented them with other heavy things that needed to be moved, the suggestions varied widely. How to move a heavy rock? "Call all the people and the dinosaurs to push," and "Take a hammer and keep chopping."

At the conclusion of her pulley story, Paley reminds us that learning is not always linear and fixed. She writes, "The adult should not underestimate the young child's tendency to revert to earlier thinking; new concepts have not been 'learned' but are only in temporary custody. They are glimpsed and tried out but are not permanent possessions."

As a role model for facilitating a problem-solving process with children, Paley is an exceptional resource, as she demonstrates in her many books. We can learn so much from her ability to listen to children's conversations, ask the right question at the right time, and allow children the time and space to try and try again.

Even her conclusion—that the children were not yet ready to fully understand and apply the concept of the pulley—demonstrates her fascination with children's thinking and the flexibility of her own expectations and ideas.

Relationships at the Heart of Problem Solving

Vivian Paley's teaching and writing also teach us that relationships are at the heart of learning and teaching. The teacher's role in facilitating problem solving depends entirely upon their ability to build supportive and trusting relationships with children.

In their book *Powerful Interactions: How to Connect with Children to Extend Their Learning*, Amy Dombro, Judy Jablon, and Charlotte Stetson (2020) present a framework for engaging with children in ways that are powerful in meaning for children and support teaching and caring relationships with adults. This framework is a useful tool for facilitating a problem-solving process in an early childhood classroom.

The framework is presented as a three-step process:

1. Be present.
2. Connect.
3. Extend learning.

Let's look at how to apply this framework to solving a problem, such as a conflict between two children over sharing a toy. Suppose you are a teacher of three-year-olds. During free play, you observe a child throwing a toy truck to the ground and yelling, "Stupid!"

STEP 1: BE PRESENT

Dombro, Jablon, and Stetson (2020, 13) explain that "to be present means pausing for just a moment to quiet your static and prepare to join the child in the interaction." This can be difficult to do when a child is yelling. Yet our ability to provide care and support to children is enhanced when we approach the problem-solving process with an open mind and an intentional physical presence—approaching children at their level and giving them your full attention.

STEP 2: CONNECT

To connect with children during a problem-solving process means listening, slowing down, and acknowledging children's feelings. Dombro, Jablon, and Stetson also remind us how important it is to personalize our interactions with children by using a child's name and home language, and by adjusting our volume and tone of voice, facial expressions, and gestures to mirror the kinds of interactions that are familiar and culturally relevant to the child. With the child who has thrown the toy truck, a teacher might address the child using an endearing nickname, "Bichito (little bug), talk to me. Tell me what you're thinking and feeling."

The teacher listens, nodding, as the child cries and says, "The truck is broken!"

"I see what you mean," the teacher replies. "It looks like one of the wheels is missing." She takes the child into her lap, they sit quietly for a moment, and then the teacher says, "Let's think about how we can solve this problem."

STEP 3: EXTEND LEARNING

Powerful interactions extend children's learning when we "help children see themselves as thinkers" (Dombro, Jablon, and Stetson 2020, 76). This idea also aligns well with the concept of a growth mindset.

In this example, the teacher uses words like *think, solve,* and *problem* in her conversation. Dombro, Jablon, and Stetson suggest that one of the important ways we can extend learning during powerful interactions is to give children time to think. In our example of the child who has thrown a toy, the teacher pauses and says, "Tell me what you're thinking and feeling." Then she waits, breathes, and allows for silence as the child thinks and gets ready to answer.

Solving problems takes time, and time is a valuable resource. You've probably heard people say, "Time is money." I would argue that in an early childhood classroom, time is even more valuable than money. Children have little use for money, but they need time to think and play, and they are rarely given enough of it.

Being a brave teacher means advocating for what children need even when there is resistance. If you are receiving pressure from supervisors, funders, or regulators telling you there is not enough time in your day to slow down and listen to children, it's time for some advocacy. Use the information and resources in this book to advocate for children and help others understand the value in taking time for active problem solving with children.

Or maybe the pressure you feel to help children move along with their problem solving is coming from inside your own head. If you question your own teaching, feeling a sense of doubt or impatience with the time and care you are taking to be present, listen to children, and gently guide their problem-solving process, then it is time to demonstrate a different kind of courage. This courage does not wear a superhero cape or skydive or climb mountains. The courage to believe in yourself is a quiet courage that grows slowly and invisibly. This is what it means to be a brave teacher. Trust yourself and trust the wisdom of following the children's lead.

CHAPTER 4

Engaging in Inquiry

In the previous chapters, we've focused, in large part, on the big ideas behind problem solving—neuroscience and cognitive development, growth mindset and resilience, and the role of the teacher. This chapter offers more practical guidance, a tool kit of questions, prompts, and ideas that teachers can keep in their back pockets, at the ready when problems arise.

Using engaging questions to guide learning is nothing new. The ancient Greek philosopher Socrates is credited with developing a process, the Socratic method, for guiding students through a series of questions that the teacher composes to help the students examine and consider a topic or idea. A more contemporary practice related to asking questions is inquiry-based learning, a form of active learning in which students form their own questions and engage in collaborative activities that explore the answers to those questions. In early childhood, when young children are still developing the ability to form their own questions, teachers may scaffold the inquiry experience by initiating and modeling the asking of questions. All these practices relate to the problem-solving process as they involve inviting children to engage with explorations and investigations in an open-ended way.

It's important to note that not all inquiries are questions. There are many ways to invite children to explore and solve a problem that do not involve asking a direct question. The act of presenting a child with a puzzle is in itself an invitation to engage in an inquiry. Sometimes there are no words to the question. In other cases, the teacher may invite conversation and inquiry by speaking but not necessarily with a question. "Tell me about what you're thinking" is more of a conversation starter than a question, yet it can lead to a very rich problem-solving process.

Likewise, not all questions are true inquiries. A closed-ended question that requires a single correct answer, such as "What is the first letter in the word *cat*?" does not invite collaborative exploration and active problem solving. Yet closed-ended questions can be turned into open-ended explorations when we focus more on the learning process and on children's feelings and opinions, such as inviting children to consider, "Which letters of the alphabet are important to your family?" Even a math question like "What is one plus one?" can be turned into an active exploration when the answer is followed by the questions, "How do you know?" and "What can we do or make that will show that one plus one is two?"

In this chapter, we'll explore ways to initiate a conversation, prompt thinking, and encourage solutions that may not be in the form of a question. We'll also look at nonverbal forms of communication and the role they too can play in the problem-solving process.

Conversation Starters

How do we show children that we're ready to listen? As described in the previous chapter, in their book *Powerful Interactions: How to Connect with Children to Extend Their Learning*, Dombro, Jablon, and Stetson advise teachers that the first step in an engaging and respectful interaction is to "be present" (2020, 13). This means to slow down, take a breath, and focus on the child. If possible, position yourself at the child's level and make eye contact or look in the same direction the child is looking, focusing your attention on whatever has caught the child's eye and demonstrating to the child that you are interested and present.

For example, let's look at a problem-solving scenario that might happen as the children settle down for naps after lunch, often a challenging transition. Everyone is worn out from a busy morning, and there's so much for teachers to do. Besides helping the children with toileting and getting on their cots, teachers might be cleaning up lunch simultaneously. The practical and logistical challenges are demanding, so it's hard to be present for a child who has a problem to solve.

> Four-year-old Elijah lies down on his cot, looking at a picture book as the other children in his preschool class prepare for nap. Suddenly Elijah sits up and begins to cry. His teacher, Diane, is across the room sweeping the floor. She puts down the broom, walks to Elijah, and kneels next to his cot.
>
> She places her hand on his shoulder and speaks in a soft voice, "I hear you crying, Elijah."
>
> Elijah continues to cry. Diane speaks again, "I'm wondering what's going on. Tell me what you're feeling."

In this scenario, the teacher has not actually asked the child a question, but she has certainly demonstrated to the child that she is present, available, and ready to help solve whatever problem has caused Elijah to cry.

Encouraging Prompts and Conversation Starters

"It looks like something important is happening here."

"It looks like there is a problem to solve here."

"Let's talk about what's going on."

"Tell me what you're thinking."

"Tell me what you're feeling."

"Tell me about this."

"I'm wondering what's going on."

"I'm wondering what you're thinking."

"I'm wondering if it's time to solve a problem."

"I'm here."

"I'm listening."

"I'm ready to help you solve this problem."

Diane's caring presence and her encouraging prompts help Elijah calm down enough to tell his teacher that he can't find his toy bunny, the one he cuddles with at naptime.

Diane replies, "That is an important problem to solve. What do you think we should do?" Elijah suggests looking in his cubby. There the bunny is found, and all is well. Diane affirms Elijah's active role in resolving the problem. "That was such a good idea. I'm so glad you were able to solve the problem," she says.

Narrating the Process

Another great strategy for initiating and facilitating a problem-solving process that doesn't necessarily involve asking a direct question is to narrate what you see as it is happening. This is also sometimes called "mirror talk" because your words are a mirror of the child's actions. Many educators (such as those trained or inspired by renowned infant specialist Magda Gerber) call this kind of narration "sportscasting" because it resembles the play-by-play descriptions of broadcasters at a sporting event. This strategy, illustrated in the following example, is especially helpful for children who struggle to speak for themselves because they are very young and still learning expressive language, are too emotional to speak, have a language delay, or are still learning the language of the classroom.

> Three-year-olds Isabella and Sophie are playing in the dramatic play corner when a conflict erupts.
>
> "Mine! I had it first!" yells Isabella as Sophie pulls on the sequined cloth in Isabella's hand.
>
> Sophie yells back, "It's my turn!"
>
> Their teacher, Ms. Brenda, is nearby. She turns and moves closer to the girls. "I hear two people who sound upset. I see you both have your hands on the sparkle vest," she says.
>
> The girls stop tugging on the cloth and look at their teacher.
>
> "It looks like we have a problem to solve," says Ms. Brenda.

In the previous example, Ms. Brenda narrates what she hears and sees. She is *mirroring* for the children what is happening so they can slow down and prepare to participate in the problem-solving process. As she facilitates the resolution of this conflict, Ms. Brenda can continue to narrate and mirror the experience for the children.

> "I had the sparkle vest first," says Isabella.
>
> "She's keeping it too long," says Sophie. "It's my turn!"
>
> "It sounds like Isabella had the vest and maybe Sophie is tired of waiting for her turn. I wonder if there's anything we can do about that," says Ms. Brenda.
>
> Isabella suggests, "She can have that one." She points to another vest.
>
> "Hmm," says Ms. Brenda. "I hear Isabella making a suggestion."
>
> Sophie replies, "I don't like that. I want this one." Sophie begins to cry.
>
> Ms. Brenda says, "I see that Sophie is crying. It's so hard to wait for a turn when there's something you really want to play with."
>
> Isabella says, "She can have it in a minute. I'm not done yet."
>
> "Oh," said Ms. Brenda. "Isabella says she will be done soon and then Sophie can have a turn. I see Sophie has stopped crying now. I wonder if maybe you've solved your problem."

By mirroring the conflict between the two children, Ms. Brenda is affirming each child's feelings and opinions. The narration also slows down the process and gives each child a chance to think and consider each step along the way.

Sentence Starters for Narrating the Process

"I see . . ."

"I hear . . ."

"I'm noticing . . ."

- "I'm watching . . ."
- "This is what I think is happening . . ."

Asking Questions

Asking children a direct question (such as, "What are you thinking?") is a core instructional practice, an essential tool in a teacher's toolbox. Each time we ask a question, we invite children to participate in a dialogue and we demonstrate our interest in their answers. And yet in my experience, I've noticed that sometimes children shy away from direct questions. They may have had negative experiences with answering questions from adults in the past. That's why prompts like "I'm wondering . . ." are often so effective. There is no demand placed on the child to answer in a certain way.

However, when asked in the context of a caring and trusting relationship, questions can begin a problem-solving process and help to define the problem, support the development of a solution, and encourage reflection on how the problem was solved (or not).

QUESTIONS THAT INITIATE

- Is there a problem we need to solve?
- What is happening?
- How do you think we might solve this problem?
- What are some ideas for solving this problem?
- Do we have everything we need to solve this problem?
- Do we need to ask for help to solve this problem?

QUESTIONS THAT SUPPORT THE PROCESS

- Are we ready to try a solution?
- What should we try first?
- What do you think we should do next?
- How is it going?
- What's happening now?

QUESTIONS THAT ENCOURAGE REFLECTION AND EVALUATION

- How did the solution work?
- Has anything changed?
- What's different now?
- Do you like this solution?
- Would you try this solution again?
- What would you do differently next time?
- If this problem happens again, what would you do?

Promoting Higher-Order Thinking

Some problems are easier to solve than others. Questions that challenge children to think with greater complexity and depth are considered to have enhanced educational value. Higher-order thinking (sometimes referred to as "HOT" for short) is thinking on a deeper and more meaningful level than just memorizing facts or relating information by rote.

The concept of higher-order thinking is often linked to the work of American educator Benjamin Bloom, who developed a taxonomy of educational objectives or, in other words, a system for classifying and measuring thinking and learning.

Bloom's taxonomy has been modified over time, but currently the categories are ordered with the simplest at the bottom and the most complex higher up:

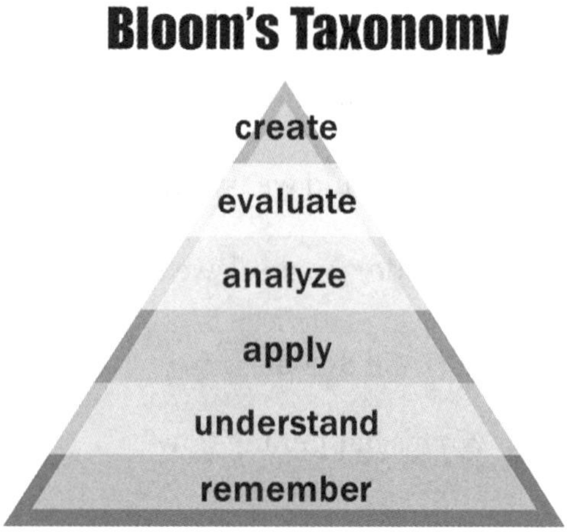

- Creating
- Evaluating
- Analyzing
- Applying
- Understanding
- Remembering

Bloom's Taxonomy

create
evaluate
analyze
apply
understand
remember

As we know from Piaget, young children are still developing the cognitive ability to think abstractly and reason with logic. Yet they can still be challenged to think creatively, and teachers can scaffold their learning to touch upon the higher-order thinking skills of applying, analyzing, and evaluating, especially when they are involved in active problem solving.

Janis Strasser and Lisa Mufson Bresson (2017) use Bloom's taxonomy as a guide for developing questions that extend children's thinking in their book *Big Questions for Young Minds: Extending Children's Thinking*. Strasser and Bresson suggest that high-level questions are not yes-or-no questions or questions with an obvious or single answer: "A high-level question is always a question that each child will answer in her own way, which indicates that she is using what she knows and what she's learning. . . . High-level questions encourage children to expand their thinking and perspective on a subject" (6).

> Five-year-old Emma is building with magnetic tiles. She has used almost every tile in the set and created a building that has two tall

> towers. Suddenly the structure shifts and collapses. Emma screams, "No!"
>
> Her teacher, Edward, approaches. "Emma, I heard a crash and a scream."
>
> Emma cries, "My castle fell down!"
>
> "Oh, no!" Edward says. "That must have been surprising."
>
> Emma nods. "I don't know how I'll ever build it again."
>
> "Hmm," says Edward. "I wonder how we'll solve that problem."

In this scenario, the teacher, Edward, can use Bloom's taxonomy as a tool to ask questions that will help Emma solve her problem and rebuild her tower.

REMEMBER

- Do you remember the shape of your castle?
- Was it wide at the bottom?
- How many towers did it have?

UNDERSTAND

- Explain to me how you built your tower.
- What did you do to build the base?
- How did you make the towers?

APPLY

- How were you able to get the tiles to stay together?
- What shapes are needed in each part of the castle?

ANALYZE

- What do you think caused the castle to fall down?

- What could you do differently this time to try to keep it from falling down?

EVALUATE

- What do you think will happen if you build it differently this time?
- Why are magnetic tiles sometimes hard to build with?
- What other materials could you use that might make your castle stronger?

CREATE

- How will you create a new structure that is even stronger?
- What new ideas will you try?

Questions That Promote Higher-Order Thinking

In general, questions that begin with *how* and *why* promote higher-order thinking because they require more than a yes-or-no or single-word answer. Another helpful question stem is "What do you think about . . ."

More examples of HOT Questions

- How will you begin solving this problem?
- How can you keep this problem from happening again?
- Why do think this is happening?
- What do you think about that?
- What can we change to make this better?

> If a child makes a mistake, my first response is always a question: "What makes you say that?" I guide them through a reasoning process, sticking with questions as much as possible so they can figure out the mistake for themselves.
>
> —F.R., early childhood educator in Ithaca, New York

Nonverbal Problem Solving

Actions speak louder than words, the saying goes, and this is true in an early childhood classroom, especially among toddlers who are just starting to learn language. Happily, talking and conversation are not the only ways to facilitate a problem-solving process with children. Very young children, children with language delays or disabilities, children who have hearing impairments, and children whose home language differs from the primary language spoken in the classroom especially benefit from nonverbal methods of communicating during a problem-solving process.

For many children, receptive language skills are more advanced than expressive language skills. Children can understand more than they can say. This means that teachers can and should speak out loud to children, even when we are focusing on nonverbal methods of communication. Many children will still benefit from hearing the teacher ask questions and narrate or mirror the child's experience. But adding a few nonverbal communication strategies to our toolboxes broadens our ability to connect with and support children.

Our ability to understand and engage with a nonverbal child depends on our ability to observe and find meaning in the child's behavior. When we observe children's play and we see a behavior or action that seems to make sense, often what we are recognizing is a *schema*. A schema is a pattern, a behavior that demonstrates exploration and understanding. According to Deb Curtis and Nadia Jaboneta (2019, 7) in *Children's Lively Minds: Schema Theory Made Visible*, "When children are exploring schemas, they are building understandings of abstract ideas, patterns, and concepts."

The schema behaviors described in *Children's Lively Minds* include these, for example:

- Transporting
- Transforming
- Enclosing and enveloping
- Connecting and disconnecting
- Positioning and ordering

Observing and understanding children's behavior in the context of these universal schema behaviors helps teachers make educated guesses at what the child is trying to accomplish and how we might help facilitate and support a problem-solving process. For example, we might observe a toddler holding two toy train cars, one in each hand. The train cars click together with a magnetic link. We see the child click the cars together and apart again and again. Her expression is serious and full of concentration, yet her body is relaxed as she repeats the same action over and over. We might be tempted to jump in and help the child, assuming that her goal is to keep the cars together and roll them across the floor. Yet an understanding of schema theory and some experience observing toddler play might help us understand that the connecting and disconnecting of the toys is not the preparation for play, it *is* the play. It is only when the child randomly turns one car around and the magnetic force is no longer pulling the cars together with a satisfying click that the child becomes frustrated and may require some support to solve that problem. In this example, the child communicates her play nonverbally through behavior, body language, and facial expression.

Let's look at another example of a situation where there are benefits to using nonverbal communication to facilitate problem solving.

> Ms. Mila's preschool class has just finished cleanup time and is preparing to go outside. When Ms. Mila grabs her jacket from the hook, a child standing nearby says, "Hey! Don't get me wet!"

> "Oh, my jacket is still wet from this morning. It was raining when I came to school," says Ms. Mila.
>
> Ms. Mila notices that Teddy, a child who has been diagnosed on the autism spectrum and rarely speaks, has a worried expression on his face. Ms. Mila approaches him and holds out her jacket for Teddy to touch.
>
> "Teddy, my jacket is still wet. Would you like to touch it and feel the water?" asks Ms. Mila.
>
> Teddy looks away, a behavior Ms. Mila recognizes as likely telling her that Teddy does not want to touch the jacket.
>
> Ms. Mila speaks to the whole class and says, "It was raining this morning. I'm wondering if it's still raining now. Hmm. How might we solve this problem?"

Ms. Mila has already engaged several strategies for nonverbal communication. She has read Teddy's facial expression to discover how he was feeling about going outside. She has used a prop—the wet jacket—to show Teddy and test her idea that he might be worried about rain. And while she has presented the problem to the class using words, she has additional strategies and tools available to engage a nonverbal child in the problem-solving process. Ms. Mila could point to the window and invite Teddy and the other children to look outside. She could use digital tools, such as a weather app on her smartphone, to show the children the weather forecast. She could arrange for Teddy and a few other children to go out to the playground to check firsthand whether it is raining.

Any of these visual, physical, and sensory strategies can help supplement problem-solving strategies to include children who are challenged to participate in conversation. A truly inclusive problem-solving experience begins with the assumption that every child has something valuable to contribute to the process. Answering questions using verbal language is just one way a child can contribute. Let us remember to welcome and pay attention to all the other wonderful ways that children contribute to the solving of interesting problems.

Greatest Hits: Our Top Twenty Favorite Questions

1. What is happening here?
2. What do you see?
3. What do you notice?
4. What do you wonder?
5. How are you feeling?
6. What are you thinking?
7. What is the problem we need to solve?
8. What are some ways we might solve this problem?
9. What do we need to do to solve this problem?
10. Whom can we ask for help?
11. What is our plan?
12. What idea should we try first?
13. How is our plan going?
14. What's happening now?
15. Has anything changed?
16. What's different now?
17. What do you think of the solution we tried?
18. Would you try this solution again?

19. What would you do differently next time?

20. If this problem happens again, what would you do?

Families, teachers, and caregivers bombard children with questions every day, from the affectionate ("How's my little love?") to the exasperated ("Why aren't you eating your vegetables?"). As facilitators of problem solving, the trick is asking questions that are meaningful to children and then, even more important, listening carefully to their answers. As author and educator Ann Pelo (2014) reminds us, "Good questions are born in silence. They begin with the humility of listening." Let's take our time throughout the process—from choosing or forming the questions, asking or inviting children to answer, waiting and supporting as children think, and listening with care to their important ideas and perspectives.

CHAPTER 5

Solving Problems Day by Day

Expect surprises. On any given day in any early childhood classroom, at least a dozen things will go wrong. Milk spills. Coteachers arrive late. Hamsters escape from their cages. Rain leaves puddles on the playground. Light bulbs burn out. Shoes are put on the wrong feet. And that's probably just the first hour of the day!

These are the everyday problems that require an optimistic approach and flexible solutions. You can expect these problems, but you can't exactly plan for them because there's always an element of surprise. So why not make the most of these surprises? Each everyday problem is actually a teachable moment.

> Once I bent down to talk to a four-year-old child who had a paintbrush in her hands. As she turned around, the paintbrush with red paint brushed across the top of my head. I pointed out that my hair had been painted and laughed. Eventually this child became more aware of where her body is in space.
>
> —N.K., preschool director in Highland Park, New Jersey

Teachable Moments

Teachable moments are spontaneous opportunities for learning that are embedded in real-life experiences. For example, suppose you are gathering a group of children around a small table for a game of Snail's Pace Race. As you set up the board, the table wobbles and tips a bit and some of the game pieces fall over. One of the children says, "Hey, stop that, naughty table!"

The wobbly table presents the opportunity for a teachable moment. You could just steady the table by sticking a small piece of cardboard under a table leg and then go on with your game. Or you could ask the children to engage in a problem-solving process that explores the concept of balance.

You might begin by saying, "Hmm. I wonder why the table is wobbling. Let's take a look." Then you might invite the children to sit on the floor and observe the legs of the table and the underside of the table as it wobbles back and forth. "What's going on here?" you might ask.

Of course, if the children are eager to engage in a problem-solving process, you may not get back to the board game that day. But the learning that will happen during this teachable moment will probably equal or exceed the learning involved in the board game.

Teachable moments are primarily facilitated through conversation. They are easiest to recognize and take advantage of in classrooms that follow predictable yet flexible routines. If the children already know the routines (such as the daily schedule) and they feel secure that their needs will be met, children (and teachers) are less thrown by surprises and more open to exploring new ideas spontaneously. For example, I wouldn't suggest stopping to fix a wobbly table on the first day of school. Children first need to feel comfortable in their environment and have a sense of trust in their teachers before they can embrace the unexpected.

Authentic Inquiry

The concept of teachable moments aligns well with inquiry-based learning and the idea behind "authentic inquiry." Judith Wells Lindfors uses the term *authentic inquiry* in her book *Children's Inquiry: Using Language to Make Sense of the World* to describe an approach to inquiry-based learning in which teachers plan for the unplanned and listen attentively to children's spontaneous questions

(1999, 51–58). It is an emergent approach to curriculum that follows children's interests and questions. Similarly, in her article "Making Sense of Experience in Preschool: Children's Encounters with Numeracy and Literacy through Inquiry," South African early childhood educator Marjorie Henningsen uses the term *authentic inquiry* to describe an "investigation that arises naturally from the interests and questions of the children as they experience the learning environment" (2013, 41). Henningsen describes how a teacher facilitated a rich learning experience for four- and five-year-olds when a doormat at the entrance to the school became excessively muddy. The children advocated for the purchase of a new doormat by writing a letter to the school director that included the specific measurements of the mat.

These spontaneous and authentic approaches to everyday problems and events involve language, literacy, and STEM learning. In my own experience, I've found that spontaneous inquiry at teachable moments works particularly well in supporting STEM learning because the everyday problems often involve messes (physics and characteristics of matter), weather (environmental science), computers and devices that don't do what you want them to do (technology), and things that are missing and broken (spatial reasoning). It's very hard to find an everyday problem that does not involve science, technology, engineering, or math.

And it is even harder to find an everyday problem that does not involve strong emotions. Every encounter with everyday problems stirs our feelings, often in uncomfortable ways. With the exception of parties and unexpected treats, most of us are not delighted by surprises. Muddy mats, broken tables, and missing spoons can create feelings of disappointment, worry, concern, and frustration. For some children, unexpected problems in the classroom may also stir up emotions associated with past and current traumas. For example, a child who has experienced harsh punishment for making mistakes at home may feel frightened when a problem arises at school.

Expressing and acknowledging feelings, for both children and adults, must be an essential priority in the problem-solving process. Learning to endure uncomfortable emotions and care for one another during challenging moments are among the most powerful lessons of the everyday problem-solving process.

Materials That Support Everyday Problem Solving

Although we can't know exactly what will go wrong in any given day, we can prepare to take advantage of the unexpected teachable moment by making sure we have tools and materials at the ready for comfort and safety, documentation, observation and measurement, and what I call "quick fix tools."

COMFORT AND SAFETY ITEMS

- Band-Aids
- ice packs
- soft toy or "stuffy"

DOCUMENTATION ITEMS

- notepad
- pen or pencil
- clipboards for children
- sticky notes
- camera, tablet, or other device for taking pictures

OBSERVATION AND MEASUREMENT ITEMS

- magnifying glass
- binoculars
- ruler
- tape measure
- flashlight

QUICK-FIX TOOLS

- tape
- screwdrivers (Phillips and flathead)
- rags or towels for spills
- batteries

You do not necessarily need to carry these items with you, but keep them available somewhere in the classroom where you can access them fairly easily.

An Everyday Problem-Solving Framework

So now you're open to surprises and prepared to take advantage of the next teachable moment that comes your way. And, of course, it doesn't take long for that opportunity to arise. For example, suppose your preschool class is transitioning outdoors to the playground, and once everyone is outside, you see that the heavy overnight rains have left the sandbox flooded. There is a large puddle at least three inches deep in the center of the sandbox area.

Here is a suggested four-step framework for solving everyday problems "in the moment."

1. Is everyone safe?
2. What's happening?
3. What can we try?
4. How did it go?

Let's look at these steps in detail.

STEP 1: IS EVERYONE SAFE?

When encountering any surprise, especially an issue related to the school facility or playground, a teacher's first concern must always be the safety of the children. In this case, the first step is keeping the children away from the sandbox until the teachers can assess the safety of the area. The teachers can position themselves next to the sandbox and tell the children, "Wait, please! We need to make sure the sandbox is safe before anyone goes in."

Even when safety is top of mind, teachers can acknowledge children's feelings in the moment: "What a big surprise! You really wanted to play in the sand, and it's hard to wait."

STEP 2: WHAT'S HAPPENING?

The second step in the problem-solving framework involves assessing what is going on and defining the problem at hand. Teachers can think out loud to help model this process. For example, a teacher might say, "I see a big puddle of water in the sandbox. I'm wondering if it's safe for children to play in the sand when there's so much water."

The children can be invited to help assess the situation too. Ask, "What do you see?" and "What do you think is happening here?" as well as more specific questions, like "Where do you think all that water came from?"

One goal of this step in the process is to name or define the problem. From a child's perspective, it isn't necessarily a problem that there is water in the sandbox. Children enjoy playing in water and wet sand. What the teachers are probably most concerned about is whether the water in the puddle is clean enough for the children to play with safely. Another issue is the quantity of water. If children are likely to get their clothes wet, the teacher must plan for changing them into dry clothes, especially if the weather is chilly.

Again, the children can be invited to participate in the naming of the problem by asking them, "I wonder what might happen if children play in the sandbox when there is such a big puddle." The teacher can use a paper or digital notebook or an audio or video recorder to document children's responses.

The naming of the problem is a significant moment in the problem-solving process. In this case, the teacher might say, “It sounds like we have a problem to solve. The rain made a big puddle in our sandbox. This puddle is too big and too dirty for children to play in the sandbox. I wonder how we will solve this problem.”

STEP 3: WHAT CAN WE TRY?

Of course, the easiest way to solve this problem is to send the children off to play in other parts of the playground. Eventually the puddle will disappear as the water is both absorbed into the sand and evaporates. Some of the sand may need to be sifted or replaced if the rainwater brought with it any hazards, dirt, or waste.

Yet some children may be very interested in taking an active role in the problem-solving process. A brainstorming session in which children think of possible solutions could take place in the moment, outdoors and next to the sandbox, or later, in a classroom meeting or as a mealtime conversation. Teachers or children could take photos of the puddle to provide a prompt and reference for the conversation.

Ask the children, “What can we do to solve this problem?” Use language that invites multiple ideas and discourages that problems have only one “correct” or “right” solution. Tell the children, “Let’s think of as many ideas as we can.”

Repeat, rephrase, and write down children’s ideas. For example, the teacher might say, “Jane says, ‘Dry it up.’ It sounds like Jane thinks we can get rid of the puddle by drying it up. That’s an interesting idea, Jane. I’m going to write that down.”

Encourage collaboration among children by helping children respond to and build on one another’s ideas: “Jane thinks we should dry up the puddle. Does anyone have an idea for how to dry it up?” Perhaps another child suggests, “An elephant could suck up the water with its trunk.” Another might say, “We can blow it with a hair dryer.” And another child might suggest, “Dry it with a big towel.”

Once everyone has had a chance to think and contribute ideas, help the children target one idea to implement: “We have lots of good ideas. Which one should we try first?”

While most children might prefer inviting a friendly elephant to visit the playground, perhaps the most practical solution involves using a big towel. The teacher might say, "Let's try it and see what happens! When we go outside after naps, we'll bring an old towel and try drying up the puddle."

While solving a problem in the moment can be exciting and engaging, it's also important for children to experience problem solving as a process that takes time. In this case, waiting until the afternoon playground session to try out the solution gives the children time to anticipate what will happen, talk about their predictions and expectations, and build interest in the problem-solving process. In this example, the passing of time also changes the size and shape of the puddle. When the children go outdoors in the afternoon, armed with a big towel, the puddle has shrunk significantly, and the teacher says, "Let's look at the puddle. What do you see? What do you think happened here?"

In this example, the teacher determines that the area is clean and safe enough for the children to enter the sandbox and use the old towel to absorb the rest of the puddle.

STEP 4: HOW DID IT GO?

The case of the shrinking puddle provides wonderful opportunities for additional conversations about the properties of water and the water cycle. The change in the puddle can be documented with before and after photos that are displayed and discussed in the classroom.

The fourth (but not necessarily final) step in the problem-solving framework is reflecting on the process by considering, "How did it go?" If the solution was not successful—if, for example, the puddle had remained large or had even grown over time—then we return to step 3 and ask, "What else can we try?" or "What solution can we try next?"

If the children are satisfied that the problem has been solved, some prompts for reflection and evaluation include these:

- "How did we solve the problem?"
- "What was something that happened that helped us solve the problem?"

- "How did that feel?"
- "What would we do differently next time?"

Documentation for the problem-solving process can include the photos, videos, and notes the teachers collect throughout the process, as well as children's drawings, emergent writing, and dictated words about their experience.

Extending beyond the Moment

An everyday problem can often become the inspiration or spark for an extended investigation or project. An emergent curriculum project can be built around answering a question that arises during the initial spontaneous problem-solving process, such as "Why did the puddle in the sandbox get smaller?" In classrooms where practices are inspired by the schools of Reggio Emilia, Italy, we talk about the environment as the third teacher. In this case, the outdoor environment, specifically the sandbox, served as a teacher that invited the children to observe and think about how water behaves in sand. Reggio-inspired educator Mary Ann Biermeier writes about the importance of the environment in developing an emergent curriculum: "Emergent curriculum is not a free-for-all. It requires that teachers actively seek out and chase the interests of the children. This kind of teaching environment demands a high degree of trust in the teacher's creative abilities, and envisions an image of the child as someone actively seeking knowledge" (Biermeier 2015).

When the questions that emerge are related to the STEM topics of science, technology, engineering, and math—as in the case of the sandbox puddle—the teachers and children become a community of researchers. It is important to provide information and resources that contribute to children's content knowledge, especially when exploring topics outside the teachers' expertise and training. In the case of the water cycle, the extension of the curriculum can include reading aloud from nonfiction picture books such as *Water Is Water* by Miranda

Paul, using digital reference tools such as Britannica Kids, and talking with water experts in your community such as municipal water engineers.

Recognizing Our Own Resistance

Teaching is hard work and solving problems takes time. It is normal and natural to resist stopping in the middle of your daily routines and predictable schedule to engage in a problem-solving process that could potentially stretch into weeks. It may be reassuring to know that a growing body of evidence from respected organizations such as the National Academies of Sciences, Engineering, and Medicine recognizes the importance of facilitated problem solving and inquiry-based learning in child development because they build a foundation of skills and dispositions that support a lifelong love of learning, especially when it comes to understanding the nature of science and how things work (National Research Council 2000).

Being open to spontaneous problem solving doesn't mean you have to stop for every problem that arises. Look for situations and ideas that link to the concepts and skills you have already identified as priorities in your classroom. For example, if your curriculum objectives include teaching children to identify shapes, skip the puddle on the playground, but the next time children are struggling to clean up the blocks in the block corner, focus on defining and facilitating problems that are related to the shapes of the blocks as well as the size and the shape of the block shelves and containers. Remember that problems are an unlimited natural resource in your classroom. If you miss capturing a teachable moment, rest assured that there are many other fascinating problems just around the corner.

CHAPTER 6

Making Friends and Getting Along

It's hard to think of something more important to a preschool child than having a friend to play with. Yet friendships are an entirely new challenge for young children. In the preschool years, children are expanding the circle of their relationships from the immediate family to wider social groups that include new children and first friendships. Social conflicts and problems with getting along are all part of typical development, the growing and learning that happen to all children during the preschool years. In this chapter, we'll examine many of the problems that typically arise between young children as they learn to make friends, such as conflicts around sharing toys and negotiating who gets to play together.

The Importance of Social-Emotional Learning

Learning to make and maintain friendships falls under the broad umbrella of social-emotional learning. The importance of social-emotional learning has been highlighted in the media, in research, and in educational programs and curricula at all levels, especially since the COVID-19 pandemic has disrupted learning and relationships in such significant ways. The Collaborative for Academic, Social, and Emotional Learning (CASEL), an organization that provides resources for educators and policy leaders, has documented the research that supports educators in prioritizing social-emotional learning as the centerpiece of strategy for supporting students during stressful and traumatic experiences (CASEL, accessed 2022). Additionally, social-emotional learning is essential for children to develop the empathy and understanding necessary for classrooms, schools, and communities to collaboratively address issues of equity.

For preschoolers, social-emotional learning begins with understanding and expressing their own emotions as well as learning to understand and listen to others. This give-and-take relationship between self and others that is at the core of social-emotional learning parallels the first two antibias goals. As mentioned in chapter 2, there are four interrelated goals of antibias education, and they relate to both children and adults. The first two goals are these:

Goal 1: Identity: "Children will demonstrate self-awareness, confidence, family pride, and positive social identities."

Goal 2: Diversity: "Children will express comfort and joy with human diversity; use accurate language for human differences; and form deep, caring connections across all dimensions of human diversity."
(Derman-Sparks and Edwards 2020, 5)

Two important competencies of CASEL's social-emotional learning framework are self-awareness and social awareness, which also are embedded in goals 1 and 2 of antibias education, reproduced above. The CASEL framework defines self-awareness as "the abilities to understand one's own emotions, thoughts, and values and how they influence behavior across contexts" (CASEL, accessed 2022). Self-awareness begins in early childhood with understanding our own feelings. This is not an easy task! Big feelings like anger and excitement can be challenging for any child, yet during the preschool years most children make great strides in learning to recognize, talk about, and manage emotions.

Developing a sense of self is also an important foundation in our ability to understand differences and to foster social awareness. The CASEL framework defines social awareness as the "abilities to understand the perspectives of and empathize with others, including those from diverse backgrounds, cultures, and contexts" (CASEL, accessed 2022).

While the first goal in an antibias education (and the competency of self-awareness) looks inward, in relation to identity, the second antibias goal (and the competency of social awareness) looks outward, in relation to diversity. These two goals are often described in terms of mirrors and windows; a mirror allows you to see yourself while a window allows you to see others. The first two antibias goals and CASEL's social-emotional learning framework are useful in thinking about and preparing to facilitate a problem-solving process among young children because they help us recognize how children are building the foundations of social-emotional learning that will support understanding and equity in school and beyond.

Learning to Talk about Feelings

Sometimes feelings are so big and overwhelming that children are not yet ready to engage in a problem-solving or conflict-resolution process. Consider a preschool child who feels frustration and hurt because another child refuses to include them and says, "You're too little to play this game!" The child may not be ready to talk about feelings that are intense or unfamiliar. Over time, through experience and with support, children will gradually gain the ability to talk and listen during a social conflict. Before the work of a collaborative problem-solving process can begin, children must have the capacity to feel big feelings without getting overwhelmed.

Parents and caregivers play a significant role in supporting children as they learn to identify, name, tolerate, and talk about their feelings. When a child is having a strong emotion that is hard to manage, especially feelings of anger, frustration, fear, or anxiety, try these strategies for supporting children in the moment:

1. Describe what you see. When children are experiencing a conflict, describe what you see in the children's body language, facial expressions, and actions. This will help build their awareness of what they and others are feeling. For

example, "Noah, I see that you are holding the tablet tightly against your chest. You're frowning and looking down at the ground. Lucas, I see your arms are crossed and there are some tears on your face. It looks like you're both having some big feelings."

2. Offer names for feelings. We can't always know exactly what another person is feeling, but we can guess and ask questions: "It looks like you're both feeling very frustrated. Are you feeling angry right now?"
3. Share your own feelings. If the children are not ready to talk about what they are feeling, tell them about your own experiences, for example, "I know what it's like to get angry. Do you remember when I spilled my cup of coffee this morning? I was so frustrated! I really wanted to drink that coffee."
4. Talk about what to do next. If you think the children might be ready to participate in a problem-solving process, let them know how you can help and give them some choices in how they might participate: "It looks like we have a problem to solve. Do you want to talk this through on your own, or shall I help?"

Remember that learning to name and manage our emotions is a lifelong process. We are planting the seeds and providing the tools to help grow both their problem-solving skills and their social and emotional skills.

Types of Social Conflicts

The nature of social conflicts is as varied and changeable as the movement of the ocean along the seashore, but there are some fairly predictable patterns to the types of conflicts that arise between children in preschool and kindergarten settings.

Conflicts in navigating friendships

Choosing someone to play with and designating someone as a "best friend" are just a couple ways children navigate their first friendships. If the other person doesn't reciprocate these overtures, or if multiple children are competing for the attention of another friend, conflicts easily arise. Name-calling and exclusion are just a few actions that escalate these conflicts and make them even harder to navigate.

Conflicts in sharing toys, materials, and spaces

When two children reach for the same toy at the same time, a conflict can easily emerge over who gets to play with it first. Figuring out how to share toys, materials, and spaces is a challenge every child encounters when playing and learning in groups.

Conflicts in negotiating roles and rules during play

When children engage in make-believe or dramatic play, such as pretending to be animals or superheroes or wizards, the negotiation of roles and rules sometimes takes more time and attention than the play itself. Who gets to take on the most coveted roles and what are the rules or events in the pretend story are major sources of conflict and negotiation during the preschool years.

Navigating Friendships

"You're not my friend anymore!" is a frequent exclamation among preschoolers as they learn how to get along—it's even the title of a book by educator Betsy Evans. In *You're Not My Friend Anymore! Illustrated Answers to Questions about Young Children's Challenging Behaviors,* Evans (2009, 4) writes, "If children could learn the skills of friendship simply by being told a rule, such as *Be friends,* the whole world would be a much friendlier place. Most children have the *desire* to be friends, but many don't have the social skills—yet—to make it happen easily."

Making friends is more an art than a science. Every relationship is different, just as every person is unique. Solving problems with young children requires flexibility all around, in both the give-and-take process of negotiating friendships required of the children as well as the flexibility and agile responsiveness required of the teacher who helps to facilitate the problem-solving process.

One of the key supports we can offer children who are struggling to resolve a social conflict is to help them understand that this is something that happens to everyone. All friends have trouble sometimes, and every relationship requires a little work. Children feel supported and affirmed when their teachers and caregivers acknowledge this challenge. For example, you might say, "I see you two are working out a problem. It's hard to get along sometimes, isn't it?" or "Friends sometimes disagree, but we can work this out."

Learning to Share

Sharing is hard. Children in groups—whether in child care, preschool, or outside of school—frequently find themselves in situations where they are asked or required to share their toys or food or the company and attention of other people.

Sharing actually requires very sophisticated skills, such as negotiation, cooperation, and taking turns. As we facilitate social conflicts around sharing, an important consideration is how we respect and honor children's choices and needs.

> We don't force children to share, but we encourage turn-taking. We teach children to ask, "Can I have a turn with your car?" and the other child can say, "You can have it when I'm done." We know that waiting is hard.
>
> We have 3s, 4s, and 5s together in one classroom. The 3s are just learning to take turns. The older children are role models. They take on a helper role. An older child might even say, "Oh, they're just learning to take turns." Having mixed ages together helps them learn patience, forgiveness, and grace. This is especially important for "only children" who don't have contact with other children at home.
>
> —K.P., C.B., and A.H., Head Start educators in Kenai, Alaska

When you find yourself in a situation where two children want the same thing, before you insist that children share, first try saying, "It looks like you both want the same toy." And instead of asking, "How can we share?" try framing the problem as one of waiting, not sharing, by saying, "It's hard to wait for a turn. Let's think of some ways you can keep yourself busy." Then allow the child who chose the toy to play as long as they like, what Sarah MacLaughlin of Zero to Three calls a "long turn." As MacLaughlin explains, "Sometimes it can feel to children that as soon as they start to play, a peer demands to 'take a turn.' It is okay to let children have a 'long turn'—a chance to play with the toy—before they share" (MacLaughlin, accessed 2022).

Negotiating Roles and Rules during Play

Would you rather be a bunny or a kitten? A robot or a ninja? A wizard or a vampire? These are just some of the important decisions children make during pretend play. Besides taking on roles, children must also decide the rules of the make-believe world they are creating. Can puppies talk? Can robots be invisible? What kind of candy do vampires eat? The excitement and importance of deciding who, what, and how to pretend is amplified by the social nature of pretend play, as these roles and rules are almost always created collaboratively with other children.

Problems that arise naturally during play will be addressed in more detail in chapter 8, but there are a few initial key ideas for teachers to think about as they support the problem-solving process during pretend play. First, remember that these negotiations are not just preparations to get ready to play but rather an essential part of the play itself. Don't rush children through the creation of roles and rules. Be patient and allow the conversations and inevitable disagreements to develop. Second, allow the children as much autonomy as possible to work out these issues on their own. If children are not hurting each other (with actions or words), let them struggle awhile with the conflicts. Wait and see whether they're able to resolve them on their own before stepping in to facilitate. Third, know that these are good problems for children to have. When discussions, conflicts, and negotiations come up during pretend play, you know the children are doing what they need to do: developing their imaginations, expanding their thinking, and figuring out how to meaningfully connect with other children.

Does an Apology Fix a Problem?

Young children are still learning to control their bodies. They bump or push each other, sometimes intentionally and sometimes purely by accident. Many families and teachers insist that when one child hurts another, an apology is in order. Other adults feel that this practice teaches children at an early age that if they say "I'm sorry" they are off the hook.

My recommendation is that when facilitating social conflicts between children, seek a process that goes beyond apologies and helps children develop feelings of empathy. Empathy is the ability to understand and relate to the feelings of others. Whether a child is made to apologize or not, the ultimate goal is to help children empathize with the experience of the other child. One way to help children develop empathy is to acknowledge and describe the feelings of the child who has been hurt. For example, a teacher might say, "I see tears on Aiden's face. He's sitting on the floor and rubbing his knee. He bumped his knee when he fell over, and now he's crying."

When a child has been hurt by another child, whether intentionally or not, sometimes the best question to ask is not, "How can we solve this problem?" but rather, "How can we help our friend feel better?" Encourage children to think of ways they can help fix whatever has gone wrong or simply offer comfort in words or actions. A child who pushed another child and caused them to fall could be enlisted to help get a Band-Aid or pick up any toys that were dropped or spilled.

Recognizing Bias in Social Conflicts

> If a child says something that is based on a bias or stereotype, such as "Boys are smart. Girls are dumb," my first response is to wonder

> what provoked or preceded this statement. Was there something that happened with a friend? This statement comes from an emotion. I'll ask the child how they feel when this statement is made.
>
> I wonder with the child about the statement. "What makes you say that?" This is an opportunity to refer back to books we read about all sorts of people and accomplishments. It is also an opportunity to talk about other issues and terms related to gender such as *transgender*.
>
> —M.D., early childhood educator in Chicago, Illinois

It's not unusual to hear children say, "That's not fair!" when they are unhappy. But not every disappointment is related to fairness. A child might protest, "No fair!" after being told it's too rainy to play outside. In this case, the child is simply disappointed. The weather isn't something we can control.

Yet sometimes conflicts arise that truly are related to fairness. For example, a child may say or show that they are choosing one playmate over another because of characteristics of identity such as gender, skin color, or differing ability. Teachers must help children solve these kinds of social problems with care and sensitivity because a child's early experiences will influence how they respond to bias and injustice in the future.

How can a teacher know when an issue between children is truly an issue of bias? Sometimes a bias is demonstrated in obvious ways, such as a child who says, "Girls are dumb!" At other times, the issues are less obvious. We may get an uneasy feeling, a sense that something is not quite right, when we notice, for example, a child who always "saves" seats for certain friends and not for others. There is no clear rule for recognizing when a conflict involves bias and inequity. As early childhood professionals, we must trust our gut and, at the same time, take responsibility for learning from experts about bias and inequities in classrooms and communities.

As mentioned earlier, an antibias curriculum approach involves four interrelated goals. The third goal is most relevant to the importance of teaching children to resolve social conflicts caused by unfairness.

Goal 3: Justice: "Children will increasingly recognize unfairness (injustice), have language to describe unfairness, and understand that unfairness hurts" (Derman-Sparks and Edwards 2020, 5).

Antibias leaders and practitioners in early childhood education suggest a variety of actions, strategies, and approaches for recognizing bias and advocating for justice. In their book *Don't Look Away: Embracing Anti-Bias Classrooms*, Iheoma Iruka, Stephanie Curenton, Tonia Durden, and Kerry-Ann Escayg (2020) remind us that antibias work begins with examining our own biases. We must be vigilant and intentional in exploring our own thinking through reading, reflection, discussion, and relationships. The more we understand our own biases, the better equipped we will be to recognize bias in our classrooms.

One helpful practice for educators in gaining a clearer understanding of the social interactions in the classroom is conducting regular observations in which we note who plays with whom and the social choices children are making. During free play or outdoor play, when children can choose where to go and with whom to play, observe and write down a few notes about what you see. Notice who initiates play and invites others to join. If you do this regularly, perhaps once a week, you'll begin to see patterns. This information will be helpful as you support children in resolving social conflicts. For example, if a problem arises because one child excludes another, you'll already have a sense of whether this is part of a pattern of exclusion or an isolated incident.

Creating or revisiting classroom rules collaboratively with children is another strategy for reducing conflicts around injustice and exclusion. As Vivian Gussin Paley (1993) demonstrated in her book *You Can't Say You Can't Play*, when the rules of the classroom prevent children from excluding others, children are better able to welcome others into their social relationships. Similarly, some schools have added "friendship benches" or "buddy benches" to their playgrounds, a place where a child can sit if they need someone to play with. When the school or the classroom community works together to create their own rules and norms around inclusion, children are much more likely to invite others into play and conversation.

Another promising practice for working to resolve social conflicts, especially those that relate to bias and equity, is designating a specific area of the classroom for working on conflicts and talking through difficult issues. The space might be a rug in a corner, a small couch, or a little tent. Some teachers call this space a *peace corner*.

> We have a peace corner in my classroom. This allows us to take a moment and process the conflicts that come up. I sit with the two children and we talk it through. Once we can say what the problem is, I'll ask, "What can we do about that?" The children can come up with ideas. Sometimes we're just not in the mood to play together, and that's okay too.
>
> For example, a child told another child, "Your skin is too dark." I tried to understand where the bias was coming from. I had a one-on-one conversation with the child, and the peace corner was a good place for that. I also involved the parent.
>
> This kind of experience can be traumatizing for the child who is hurt by those words. I also use picture books to address these feelings and help nurture a sense of empathy for others.
>
> —S.G., pre-K teacher in Chicago, Illinois

Picture Books That Challenge Assumptions and Stereotypes

Books have a way of sparking conversation and opening minds that can be even more powerful than ordinary conversation. When we read an illustrated story to children, we share an experience that is meaningful yet safe and entertaining. Here are suggestions of books that can spark conversations about fairness, feelings, and friendships.

Picture books about fairness

And Tango Makes Three by Justin Richardson and Peter Parnell

Brave Irene by William Steig

A Chair for My Mother by Vera B. Williams

I Love My Purse by Belle DeMont

Julián Is a Mermaid by Jessica Love

Milo Imagines the World by Matt de la Peña

Mixed: A Colorful Story by Arree Chung

Pink Is for Boys by Robb Pearlman

The Story of Ferdinand by Munro Leaf

Picture books about feelings

The Feelings Book by Todd Parr

Give Me Back My Book! by Travis Foster

How Are You Peeling? Foods with Moods by Saxton Freymann

How Do Dinosaurs Say I'm Mad? by Jane Yolen

Llama Llama Mad at Mama by Anna Dewdney

Wemberly Worried by Kevin Henkes

When Sophie Gets Angry—Really, Really Angry . . . by Molly Bang

Picture books about friendships

Ash Dresses Her Friends by Fu Wenzheng

Can I Play, Too? by Mo Willems

The Farmer and the Clown by Marla Frazee

Frog and Toad Are Friends by Arnold Lobel

Good News, Bad News by Jeff Mack

I Just Ate My Friend by Heidi McKinnon

Little Blue and Little Yellow by Leo Lionni

My Friends by Taro Gomi

The Rabbit Listened by Cori Doerrfeld

A Friendship Problem-Solving Framework

The problem-solving framework suggested in the previous chapter can also be useful in facilitating a social conflict between children, with special care and extra time devoted to listening to each other and acknowledging feelings.

Here is a suggested four-step framework for solving friendship problems "in the moment."

1. Is everyone safe?
2. What's happening?
3. What can we try?
4. How did it go?

STEP 1: IS EVERYONE SAFE?

In social conflicts, ensuring children's safety means protecting children from both physical and emotional harm. In early childhood classrooms, "no hurting" is the most important rule. Sometimes teachers must step in and separate children if they are hitting or hurting each other. Similarly, if children are calling each other names or saying other hurtful things to each other, it is the teacher's role to intervene. "I won't let you hurt each other" is a brief and direct explanation when you step in to help resolve a conflict. If everyone is safe, the process can slow down, and children can be drawn into taking active roles in solving the problem.

STEP 2: WHAT'S HAPPENING?

Again, thinking out loud and describing what you see help teach children to recognize and express their own feelings and begin to understand the feelings of others. Describing what you see also slows down the process and gives children a chance to catch their breath and calm down. You might say, for example, "I see

Riley has her hand on the chair where Ava is trying to sit down. Both of you are frowning and looking angry. I'm wondering what's happening here."

Ask open-ended questions that help the children express their feelings, explain their position, and define the problem that needs to be solved, such as "What are you feeling?" or "What are you hoping will happen?"

Summarize your understanding of what happened: "Here's what I think the problem might be. It sounds like Ava wants to sit next to Riley, but Riley was saving this chair for someone else. Is that what happened?" and "I wonder what we can do to solve this problem."

STEP 3: WHAT CAN WE TRY?

When resolving a conflict between two children or among several children, it's important that each child is given an opportunity to speak and contribute to the problem-solving process. You might say, for example, "I'm going to give each of you a chance to talk. What can we do to solve this problem?"

In negotiating a situation where one child was "saving" the chair for another, you might connect the situation to issues of fairness and equity that may already be expressed in your classroom rules or norms. If this is the first time that "saving" a space has come up, the solution to the problem might involve bringing the issue to the whole class to discuss. For example, you might say, "Ava, it sounds like you're saying it's not fair to save an empty chair. You think there should be a rule about this. Let's ask the rest of the class at circle time."

As the teacher and the moderator of the conflict, don't be afraid to step in and assert your authority in resolving the conflict, for example: "Riley, please move your hand so Ava can sit down. We'll all have a chance to talk more about whether or not people can save chairs when we meet together as a class." The important thing is engaging children to actively participate in the process, even if they are not given the power to make the final decision.

STEP 4: HOW DID IT GO?

In the conflict over "saving" the chair, the whole class can be invited to reflect on what happened and participate in a discussion about how the classroom community will solve problems like this in the future. The issue can be discussed without naming or shaming specific children.

You might begin by saying something like, "I'm noticing that sometimes people are 'saving' the seat next to them and not letting anyone sit there. I'm wondering if this is fair. Is it okay to save seats?" Be ready to take more time and continue the discussion or revisit the issue later.

Helping young children solve social problems can be very challenging. Hurt feelings are much harder to understand and talk about than broken toys or spilled milk. Even as adults, there's so much to learn about feelings and friendships and how to get along well with others. Social-emotional learning is a work in progress, and we all must strive for growth and learning over easy and quick solutions. As we've seen throughout the problem-solving process, it's all about the journey.

CHAPTER 7

Communicating to Solve Problems

Most of the problem-solving strategies discussed in this book require verbal communication, such as asking open-ended questions to facilitate a problem-solving conversation among children.

- What about children who are still learning the language and vocabulary necessary to participate in a problem-solving process?
- What about children who have talents and skills to contribute to the problem-solving process but who express their ideas in other ways besides verbal language?
- What about the actual problems that are caused or worsened by miscommunication and misunderstandings?

In this chapter, we'll explore all three questions as we examine ways to support language learners, honor multiple methods of communication, and facilitate the resolution of miscommunications and misunderstanding.

Preschool Milestones in Language Development

It may help to remind ourselves that all preschoolers, children between the ages of two and five, still have so much to learn about language and communication, and language development typically progresses at a very rapid pace during these important years. Claudina Hannon of the CDA Council for Professional Recognition reminds us that making mistakes is part of the learning process. "When children use incorrect grammar during this stage, rather than correct them, help them by responding with correct grammar as you have a conversation. If a child says, 'I color orange frog,' you can respond with 'Yes, I see you have colored the frog orange'" (Hannon, accessed 2022).

According to the American Speech-Language-Hearing Association (ASHA, accessed 2022), some milestones of typical development in language during the preschool years include these:

AGES 2–3

- Put two or three words together, like "big dog nice."
- Use words like *in, on,* and *under* that show location.
- Asks questions such as "Mine?" or "Why?"

AGES 3–4

- Can answer simple questions such as, "Where's your shoe?"
- Uses pronouns like *I, you, me, we,* and *they*.
- Uses some plural words, like *cars, trees,* and *chairs*.
- May make some mistakes in grammar, like "I running fast."

AGES 4–5

- Learns to name letters and numbers.

- Uses longer sentences that have more than one part, such as "I can jump, and I can swim."
- May make some mistakes in grammar, like "Sophie gots two dogs, but I gots just one."

Language Delays and Other Communication Challenges

In an inclusive classroom, every learner is welcome and has opportunities to thrive. Children who experience challenges with language and verbal communication should always be invited to join in problem-solving experiences in the classroom—not just included but welcomed as active participants and problem solvers.

Causes of language delays can include hearing impairments, autism spectrum disorders, and cerebral palsy as well as social and emotional issues such as trauma. Delays, disabilities, and difficulties with language may affect both *receptive* language, how a child understands the communications received from others, and *expressive* language, the language the child communicates to express ideas and emotions. Our receptive language vocabulary is generally larger than that of our expressive language.

Children with language delays, disabilities, and difficulties may have trouble answering and asking questions, describing new and novel ideas, and speaking up in a group, all frequent elements of a collaborative problem-solving process. These children need additional supports from their teachers to fully participate in a problem-solving process. *Total communication* is an effective strategy for improving communication in a classroom with very diverse abilities. Rather than just relying on one way of communicating, the total communication approach combines several methods, including nonverbal (body movements, demonstration), language (speech, sign language), and symbols (drawings, props). The powerful idea behind total communication is that using multiple methods of communication gives children multiple opportunities to understand and engage.

Support All Language Learners

The term *language learner* is often used in relation to bilingual or multilingual children, but aren't we all language learners? Just the other day I learned the meaning of the word *zhuzh*, which is to make something more interesting or attractive by changing it slightly or adding to it. I'm still learning new vocabulary words and new ways of expressing myself, even though my formal schooling ended decades ago. I am a language learner.

Children are considered dual-language learners or multilanguage learners, when, for example, a child is learning Spanish from their family at home and learning English in their preschool classroom. According to the WIDA Consortium, young dual-language learners may learn multiple languages simultaneously from birth when multiple languages are spoken in the home. Or they may learn multiple languages sequentially, such as adding English to their home languages when they enter preschool (WIDA 2020).

Many experts in dual-language learning recommend that teachers learn to say ten to twenty key words in each child's home language to help them feel welcome, safe, and comfortable starting from their first day. This strategy can be tailored to support the problem-solving process when you add problem-solving vocabulary and phrases to the list.

Use a digital tool like Google Translate or ask a bilingual staff or community member to help translate problem-solving words and phrases such as the following:

- "We have a problem to solve."
- "Let's think about this."
- "What are your ideas?"
- "Can you show me?"

Nonverbal Problem Solving

Loris Malaguzzi, one of the founders of the acclaimed infant-toddler centers and preschools of Reggio Emilia, wrote, "The child has a hundred languages, a hundred hands, a hundred thoughts, a hundred ways of thinking, of playing, of speaking. A hundred always a hundred ways of listening" (Malaguzzi, accessed 2022). For Reggio-inspired educators, the concept of the hundred languages means we recognize that children communicate in more ways than just spoken words. Children show us what they know and how they feel through play; through movement and gesture; through media like drawing, painting, and clay; and even through digital tools.

We can apply the concept of the hundred languages of children to the problem-solving process by encouraging children to communicate, experiment, and reflect using a wide variety of methods and media. Experimenting with multimedia communication and nonverbal methods of expression in an early childhood classroom benefits all students, and it is of particular value to children who struggle with verbal communication.

MOVEMENT AND GESTURES

Most teachers of young children are already pretty adept at reading children's body language and facial expressions. We can apply these skills to support all children's active participation and collaboration during problem-solving conversations. When children are nonverbal or struggling to express their ideas, we can validate children's movements, facial expressions, and gestures. For example, you might say, "I see Paul pointing to that big box. Let's look inside and see what's in there." By acknowledging these nonverbal contributions to the conversation, we are showing all the children that everyone has something important to add to the problem-solving process.

One of the most powerful ways we can do this is by intentionally shifting our invitation of "Tell me . . ." to include "Show me . . ."

- "Show me what's happening here."

- "Show me your idea for solving this problem."
- "Show me how you feel about this solution."

Be sure to add or exaggerate your own movement, expressions, and gestures. Tap your head to show that you're thinking. Tilt your head to show that you're wondering. Put your hand to your ear to show that you're listening.

ROLE PLAY AND PRETENDING

Like the classic party game of charades, which challenges us to act out words and ideas, we can demonstrate the parts of a problem-solving process using role playing or, in the vocabulary of early childhood, by pretending.

Suppose a teacher is working with a pair of children to resolve a conflict over a set of blocks. One child wants to play with the blocks on the floor, and the other child wants to play with the blocks on the table. One way to help the children consider various solutions is to act out some potential ideas.

"Let's pretend that I'm playing with the blocks on the table," the teacher says. The teacher then pantomimes what that might look like, followed by, "Now let's pretend that I'm playing with the blocks on the floor." The physical movement of acting out the two options might help the children evaluate the choices in ways that words alone would not allow. In this scenario, the children will be able to see which option will allow for more space to spread out.

Children can be invited to participate in a pretend demonstration or role-playing session as a regular part of the class problem-solving process. For example, a preschool class is preparing to walk to a nearby park for a picnic lunch, but the wagon they usually use to carry the lunches has been borrowed by another class. As the class brainstorms ideas for how to carry the food, some silly and some practical, the children can be invited to "pretend" or demonstrate their ideas.

"Put all the lunches in a really big backpack."

"We'll carry the lunches on our heads!"

"Drive the lunches in a car."

PROPS, DOLLS, AND PUPPETS

Using physical objects can demonstrate or test ideas as well as spark new ones. The previous example involving lunches can be extended by using props to test the ideas, such as backpacks of various sizes. The containers can be measured or tested to see how many lunches they might hold. Using props in this way is especially helpful for children who are dual-language learners or who have communication challenges.

Another similar strategy is using dolls or puppets to act out ideas and plans or to "speak" to the children. A particular practice in early childhood education uses persona dolls to talk about challenging or sensitive topics. A persona doll is a special doll a teacher uses to introduce new ideas and concepts to children. For example, a teacher might bring a persona doll to morning circle time, introduce the doll by name, and tell the children a story about the doll's experience in the world. The story might have a meaningful connection to a current struggle or issue relevant to the children. For example, the teacher may explain that the persona doll is feeling nervous about going to kindergarten or feeling sad about the recent death of a pet. In their article "Problem Solving with Young Children Using Persona Dolls," Jan Pierce and Cheryl Lynn Johnson (2010, 106) explain that "persona dolls are used by early childhood educators to solve problems and teach inclusive social and emotional skills." Persona doll researchers and practitioners have found that children are generally more open to discussing strong feelings and sensitive subjects when speaking with or about a doll.

While I don't have specific training or experience using persona dolls, I have frequently used dolls and puppets with preschool children to support problem-solving discussions. A child who is feeling left out of a play situation will feel affirmed when the teacher's puppet says, "I'm so sad. I don't have anyone to play with." I've found that a doll or puppet is especially effective during a class discussion when we are talking over classroom rules, such as whether to allow children to "save seats." Children seem to be much more attentive when the puppet is the one to say, "I feel left out when I can't sit next to my friend."

Consider setting aside one special doll or puppet to use during problem-solving sessions. Give the doll or puppet a name and find a comfortable place for it to sit or rest when not in use. When problems arise, this special friend will be ready to listen to children and reflect their feelings.

PHOTOS, ILLUSTRATIONS, AND GRAPHICS

A picture communication board supports language learners and is also useful to all children when facilitating a problem-solving process. Create a picture board that demonstrates the key steps and questions you've established (or plan to establish) in your classroom for problem solving and conflict resolution. For example, find images such as photos or drawings that illustrate the statements:

- "We have a problem to solve."
- "I have an idea."
- "I like your idea."
- "Let's try something else."

You can also include pictures or emojis that represent feelings such as *happy, sad, worried, excited, angry,* and *peaceful.*

Demonstrate how to use the picture board by pointing to specific images. Encourage children to use the picture board to communicate during a problem-solving process.

Misunderstandings and Miscommunications

I have a confession. I've never really liked TV shows and other kinds of media that make fun of children's mistakes. The classic example is the show *Kids Say the Darndest Things,* but there are plenty of instances on social media of parents posting about the funny mistakes their children make. It's not that these clips and stories aren't funny. Some are actually hilarious. What bothers me is that most of the time the children are too young to have any say in how their experience is shared with others, especially in such a public forum. And there's rarely any acknowledgment of how the child's mistake is part of a positive learning and growing process. That said, I will share with you a story of a child's funny mistake from the early years of my teaching experience, but I've changed the name of the child to protect their privacy, and I will include a discussion of the context and the learning that came later.

A small group of children in my preschool class decided to make a train by putting chairs in a row. The chair in front was the engine, and the chair in back was the caboose. The children also cut some construction paper into small pieces to make the tickets. Once everything was ready to go, they invited me to ride on the train. I bought a ticket and took my seat. When Jack, the train conductor came by, I asked, "Aren't you going to punch my ticket?" Jack grinned widely, made a fist, and punched my ticket as hard as he could. I almost fell off my chair! I quickly realized that my understanding of *punch* differed from Jack's understanding of the word. Once I recovered, I found a hole punch in the art corner and showed Jack how to punch a hole in each train ticket.

I still smile when I remember that story, a great example of the types of misunderstandings that typically happen as children learn language. But some communication problems that arise in early childhood classrooms are nothing to smile about. I recall a child who insisted there was a "bow-lee" on the playground, and it took me weeks to figure out she was trying to tell me that someone was bullying her.

Often the miscommunication is between children, rather than between a teacher and child—these problems require special care and sensitivity in facilitating a solution. Take, for example, a child who is crying because another child said, "You're too gay." Is this an example of bias, or is this a miscommunication?

Many of the problem-solving strategies proposed in previous chapters can be applied to this type of situation as well. The initial priority is to ensure children's safety. In this case, safety means emotional safety, or reassurance that the children's feelings are important and that the teacher is ready and available to help support both children.

> My first response would always be a question (in an inquisitive, not accusatory tone): "What makes you say that?" Their answer will let

> you know whether it's a mistaken idea or a mistake in language or something else. From there, I'd guide them through a reasoning process, sticking with questions as much as possible so they can figure out the mistake for themselves.
>
> —M.D., early childhood educator in Chicago, Illinois

Defining and solving the problem means unpacking what the words *You're too gay*, mean to each child. As the teacher, I would begin by saying, "I don't know what *You're too gay* means, but I can see that someone is upset, so let's figure this out." Next, I would take both children aside, perhaps in a classroom peace corner, for a quiet conversation.

One of the amazing things about the way children learn language is that they usually have a tremendous capacity to repeat the words and phrases they have heard from others. Children often use words they don't fully understand, and they often use words incorrectly. When this happens, when children are experimenting with language in new ways, they also are unlikely to have the vocabulary to fully explain to you what they meant.

In this example of a child who says, "You're too gay," it may be most helpful to focus on feelings rather than definitions. Define the problem as "Someone's feelings are hurt, and they're crying." Then ask, "What can we do to solve this problem?" If the child who spoke those words didn't understand what they were saying, and this is truly a misunderstanding, then this opens a path to move forward. That child might not be able to say, "I didn't mean to make you cry," but they might be able to say, "Let's play something else," or make some kind of caring gesture that will make the crying child feel better.

When miscommunications or misunderstandings touch upon sensitive topics or potential bias, it's important to follow up by talking individually and discreetly with the families of each child. They may have some insights and background about the meaning of the exchange.

Communication is essential to all kinds of problem solving—everyday problems, social conflicts, problems that arise during play, and so on. It's important to have strategies in your tool kit that go beyond facilitating verbal conversations. All young children are still new to using words to solve problems, and many are struggling just to find their voices. Strategies that communicate using the hundred languages and allow space for mistakes will expand our opportunities to connect and solve problems together.

CHAPTER 8

Playing with Problems

Among my favorite problems are those that emerge from children's play. The children truly own these problems, as they grow directly out of their own decisions, actions, and imaginations. We can think about play as fitting into several categories:

- Pretend play (also known as "dramatic play" or "fantasy play")
- Outdoor play (active play, playground play, nature play)
- Sensory play (sand, water, clay, and so forth)
- Creative arts (drawing, painting, dance, music)
- Construction play (building with blocks and other materials)
- Games (board games, card games, manipulatives)

Within each category of play, there are countless ways for things to go wrong, more than can be documented in a single book. All categories of play involve problems that children must solve using their bodies, minds, and spirits. For our purposes, let's group together outdoor play, sensory play, and creative arts as we focus on the problems children solve with their bodies—by running and climbing outdoors; by using their hands and tools to explore sensory materials; and by the physical movements involved in creating works of art, dancing, or playing music. Let's also group together construction play and games as we focus on the problems children solve with their minds—the cognitive challenges that involve STEM learning and understanding the rules and structures of games. But first, let's focus on one very special category of play—pretend play—and the kinds of problems children solve with their imaginations.

Problems Children Solve with Their Imaginations

Babies don't pretend. To pretend requires cognitive growth and development to the point that you can imagine something in your mind that doesn't exist in real life. A toddler clomps around in her daddy's snow boots, imagining that someday she will be big enough to shovel the snow just like her parents. In preschool, the golden age of pretending, children routinely create elaborate pretend scenarios. They are not just mommies and daddies; they are puppies and tigers, dragons and fairies, superheroes and wizards. Vivian Gussin Paley (2004, 8) writes in *A Child's Work: The Importance of Fantasy Play* that this type of play "is the glue that binds together all other pursuits" in the preschool classroom.

When a problem develops during pretend play, before teachers jump in to help resolve the problem, I advise them first to ask themselves, "Is this problem happening inside the story or outside the story?" By *story* I mean the pretend world the children have created in their imaginations.

A problem *outside* the story typically happens before the real pretending begins and often involves issues of inclusion and exclusion. Someone wants to play and the others might not let them. This is the type of social problem discussed in chapter 6.

A problem *inside* the story is something that adds to the drama of the pretend scenario, such as when a child who is pretending to be a wizard declares that she has cast a spell on another child and turned them into a frog, but the other child says, "I don't want to be a frog." This is a conflict around what will happen next within the pretend world the children are creating.

I recommend that teachers generally avoid intervening when the problem occurs within the story unless safety is an issue. The children used their imaginations to create the problem, and usually they can use their imaginations to resolve the problem. With the wizard's spell, the children now have an opportunity to negotiate. Perhaps the wizard will try a new spell that turns their friend into a unicorn and finds that this new spell is much more welcome.

At times a teacher must intervene in a problem that arises during pretend play for children's safety. Whenever possible, try to address the issue from inside the story, honoring the pretend world the children have created. For example, I once observed one of my coteachers rush into the dramatic play corner when she saw a child climbing on top of the play stove. Holding the child to keep her from falling, she said, "Let's keep you safe. I don't want you to burn your feet on the hot stove."

Vivian Paley quotes her mentor, educator Rena Wilson, as offering this advice: "Pretend *you* are the children who are playing. What are you trying to accomplish and what stands in your way? . . . Remind yourselves of what it was like to be a child" (Paley 2004, 2).

Sometimes children ask a teacher for assistance when the play scenario has run aground and conflicts seem too difficult to overcome. Then mediation is in order. The teacher can serve as a mediator without taking on a pretend role. Suppose a conflict arises because three children are pretending to be fairies but only one sparkly fairy wand is available. Fairy voices are raised, and an argument is brewing. Many of the conversation starters and engaging questions discussed in chapter 4 work well in facilitating problems that occur during pretend play.

The conversation begins with the universal "It looks like something important is happening here."

The technique described in chapter 4 as "narrating the process" can be tailored to include and acknowledge the children's pretend roles and imagined setting. In the scenario with the three fairies but only one fairy wand, the teacher might say, "It sounds like there are three fairies and only one magic wand. What can we do to solve this problem? Do any of the fairies have ideas?"

While the negotiation could focus on the ordinary considerations of classroom turn-taking, the children's pretend scenario provides some new avenues for pursuing solutions. For example, the teacher might ask, "Are there any other objects here that might have magical powers?"

A question like this, which incorporates the children's imaginary world into the problem-solving process, could expand the children's thinking and generate new solutions to consider. With any luck, the solution to the problem might look like three fairies, one with a magic wand, one with a magic necklace, and one with magic shoes.

Paley wrote, "It is in the development of their themes and characters and plots that children explain their thinking" (2004, 8). As teachers, we can honor children's creativity and ideas by calling them to use their own imaginations to solve the problems that arise during play.

Problems Children Solve with Their Bodies

Outdoor play, sensory play, and the creative arts include such a broad array of play experiences that it's hard to narrow our discussion to just one type of problem solving. But what all these types of play have in common is an element of physical movement, sometimes large-motor and sometimes small-motor. And another commonality that comes with physical play is the necessity of risk: the physical risk that comes with running and climbing and big body play; the risk of messes and spills that comes with sensory play; and the creative risks of making art, dancing, and playing music.

OUTDOOR PLAY

Playgrounds in the United States, especially those in licensed child care centers, must meet stringent requirements for safety. Advances in the design and materials used in the fall zones under playground equipment have significantly reduced playground injuries. At the same time, from the 1970s through the 1990s, an increase in injury-related lawsuits convinced policy makers that playgrounds should not allow for any level of risk.

In the twenty-first century, the pendulum began to swing back in the other direction as a growing body of research revealed that some risky outdoor play can promote children's healthy development. For example, in 2011, Ellen

Sandseter, a professor of early childhood education at Queen Maud University College, published the paper "Children's Risky Play from an Evolutionary Perspective: The Anti-Phobic Effects of Thrilling Experiences" with coauthor Leif Kennair. The paper identifies different kinds of risky play:

- Exploring heights
- Handling dangerous tools
- Being near dangerous elements, such as fire
- Rough-and-tumble play
- Speed
- Exploring on one's own/disappearing

The research suggests that children need physical exercise that tests their limits. Important social-emotional learning is associated with risk. But what children need to experience is not danger but fear. They need to *feel* that what they are doing is dangerous. They need to feel the fear and then overcome it. The documentary film *The Land* features an adventure playground in Wales where children are allowed to swing from ropes, climb on old barrels, use tools to build whatever they want out of scraps of wood, and even build their own fires. In the film, one worker explains the difference between a risk and a hazard: "Risks and hazards are different things. A risk is something they're choosing to interact with" (Boston Children's Museum 2016). This distinction between a risk and a hazard is helpful to teachers, parents, and caregivers. We must be vigilant to protect children from hazards like harmful chemicals or electrical cords in children's play spaces. But we can allow children to experience a sense of danger as they take small risks during active play, such as balancing on logs or jumping over rocks.

What does all this talk of risks, dangers, and hazards have to do with problem solving? Let's think about what kinds of problems occur when preschoolers play outdoors. We see social conflicts and communication problems of the ilk addressed in chapters 6 and 7, certainly, and everyday problems, such as those described in chapter 5.

But what's unique about the problems that arise outdoors is that they often revolve around disagreements about what is considered safe, both disagreements between teachers and children and disagreements between children. For example, one day one of my preschool students decided she wanted to climb a tree on our playground. She tried to shimmy up the trunk, but she wasn't able to get very high. So she rolled a tricycle over to the base of the tree and was about to stand on the seat of the trike, probably hoping that she might reach one of the lower branches of the tree. I didn't think that looked very safe. I stopped her from standing on the seat of the trike and said, "Let's talk about this. What's your plan here?"

Our ethical responsibilities as early childhood educators call us to prioritize children's safety. We must protect children from hazards, but we must allow children to experience risk.

When we're sure children are not safe, we say, "Stop!" But when we're not sure, we say, "Be careful." But what do children hear when we say "Be careful"? It's complicated. Part of what we communicate when we say "Be careful" is "I care about you, and I don't want you to get hurt." But I also think that at least part of what we communicate to children when we say "Be careful" is, "I don't know if I can trust you to do what you're doing." I would argue that saying the words *Be careful* doesn't actually help children be careful. I suggest it might be more useful to ask a question that empowers the child to become more focused on what they're doing. We can ask questions like the following:

- "Are you safe?"
- "Do you feel safe?"
- "Do you need any help to stay safe?"
- "Do you feel ready to do this?"
- "What do you need to do to stay safe right now?"

We can also tell children directly what we hope they will do and feel:

- "It's important to know how to be safe."

- "You can learn how to make good decisions about what your body can do."
- "Listen to your body. You can learn to feel when something is safe and right."
- "If you feel strong and ready, do it!"

When problems arise, it's important to allow children to assess their own risk and incorporate those considerations into the problem-solving process.

SENSORY PLAY

Sensory play refers to hands-on, messy play with open-ended materials such as these:

- water
- sand
- mud
- clay
- playdough
- shaving cream
- fingerpaint

Much of the pleasure of this type of play comes from the way it engages our senses, primarily touch, but also sight, smell, sound, and even occasionally taste.

The problems that arise during sensory play are usually related to messes and spills. Splashes and spills are a given during any messy sensory play, and solving these problems is an integral part of the learning. Some children are not as comfortable as others with messy play, and a problem might arise, for example, when a cautious child accidentally splashes a bit of mud on their clothing.

The problem-solving process will probably include brainstorming solutions to the muddy clothes, but don't miss the opportunities for discovery and reflection inherent in sensory play. A child-centered approach to problem solving that empowers children as active learners highlights the child's role in the phenomenon they are observing and experiencing. The early childhood literature often focuses on the science learning related to the properties of matter, liquids, and solids. Less often addressed is the topic of force as it relates to the children's physical movements. We are accustomed to drawing children's attention to the materials themselves—"What's happening to the water? To the sand?"—and less accustomed to drawing children's attention to their own movements that have caused the water or sand to change—"How are you moving your hands and fingers? What do you see? What do you feel? What do you smell?"

As children work to solve a problem, teachers can help them analyze what happened using their own bodies. With the mud splash, have the child step away from the mud and ask, "Can you show me how you moved your hand to make the water splash like that?" Discuss the details, such as, "How fast did you move?" or "How close was your hand to the mud?"

CREATIVE ARTS

The other chapters in this book address many kinds of problems that might arise when children are participating in the arts, such as an everyday, practical problem like a missing paintbrush. But some problems that arise during creative arts happen because a child has taken a creative risk.

For example, I once observed a child making a collage. She completely covered the paper with glue, glitter, and sequins. Then she did it again, adding another layer on top of the first. And then she did it again, and then again, until her collage was almost an inch thick. Throughout the gluing process she was completely silent and absorbed. It seemed she was deeply engaged in her creative process. But when she finished and tried to lift the collage to place it on the drying shelf, it fell apart.

Let's think carefully about how to define this problem. Did the child use too many collage items or add too many layers? Or was the collage paper not strong enough to hold her vision for her work of art? Consider great artists like Jackson Pollock, groundbreaking visionaries who challenged us to rethink how we define art. Perhaps this child will one day become a visionary artist as well. In the case of the heavy collage, this child seemed happy with the results of her work. When it fell apart, she pressed it back together and placed it in a plastic bag. She seemed less concerned with maintaining the original shape of the art and more concerned with keeping all the pieces together, contained in one place. She took the bag of soggy collage home, proud and satisfied.

Allow children to take creative risks. Take care not to define the problems that arise as stemming from a child's work being "too much" or "too loud." Encourage children to take creative risks, even if they result in problems.

Problems Children Solve with Their Minds

Building with blocks, designing patterns with colorful parquetry tiles, creating pictures with tangrams, putting puzzles together—these play experiences all support children's cognitive development, especially in the areas associated with STEM. Construction toys, manipulatives, and puzzles are designed to intentionally create problems for children and challenge them to resolve those problems through play, experimentation, and reasoning.

> If I'm building a tower and it keeps falling down, I make it again and again.
>
> —Elise, five years old

I find block play and other kinds of construction play particularly valuable and fascinating because of the ways these experiences challenge children to solve problems in three dimensions. It's one thing to put together a flat puzzle, but it's a whole new challenge to build a block structure that climbs into the sky. And 3-D structures fall apart in spectacular ways that are sure to capture our attention.

Early childhood educator Rosanne Regan Hansel focuses on the value of 3-D play in her book *Exploring the 3-D World: Developing Spatial and Math Skills in Young Children*. She explains how construction play is inherently iterative, meaning the children's structures can be rebuilt, added to, changed, or adapted, noting that "learning is iterative when children actively explore materials to build new knowledge and then test and revise their ideas and theories with teacher guidance" (Hansel 2021, 33).

DESIGN ENGINEERING IN THE BLOCK CORNER

When children build and put things together, the play space becomes a laboratory, and the children become scientists and engineers. The teacher's role is to facilitate in ways that deepen and extend children's learning. As mentioned in chapter 2, understanding a design engineering framework helps teachers know how and when to guide play and support children in taking an active role in a problem-solving process.

For example, suppose a child is building a house using wooden unit blocks. She places a block across the top of the structure, but the roof keeps falling in. A design engineering process can be used to shape the questions, conversations, and actions as the teacher gently facilitates and the child takes the leading role in solving the problem.

The process begins with a question. Ideally, the child poses the question, but the teacher can help scaffold by rephrasing the child's ideas and feelings.

> CHILD: I can't make this stupid roof stay on!
>
> TEACHER: It sounds like you're feeling pretty frustrated. What are you trying to figure out?
>
> CHILD: I need the roof to stay.
>
> TEACHER: Okay. How can you build a strong roof that won't fall in?

The next step in the design engineering process involves imagining many ways to answer the question or solve the problem.

> TEACHER: What's one new idea you could try?
>
> CHILD: I don't know.
>
> TEACHER: Are there other blocks you could try? Look around. Do you see anything you haven't tried yet?

CHILD: I could try the planks or the sticks.

TEACHER: Those are two good ideas!

Next, design engineers plan for their first iteration or solution.

TEACHER: Which will you try first—planks or sticks?

CHILD: I'll try the sticks.

TEACHER: Okay. Why did you choose the sticks?

CHILD: They're longer.

TEACHER: So you need something long. Tell me more. Why do you need something long to make the roof?

CHILD: Because it has to fit the whole thing.

Next we practice the most active step in the design engineering process, implementing the plan and creating a solution, or at least attempting to solve the problem for the first time.

TEACHER: I see how you're adding the sticks to the house. You're lining them up side by side.

CHILD: (*nods*)

Finally it's time to evaluate and test the solution.

TEACHER: How are you doing? Did the sticks work well?

CHILD: They stayed up.

TEACHER: Okay, so the sticks didn't fall in. That's good.

CHILD: But I can still see some holes.

TEACHER: So you're noticing there are some gaps between the sticks. Do you want to work on that or are you okay with it?

CHILD: I'm okay with it.

THE SCIENTIFIC METHOD

A design engineering process is very similar to what's known as the "scientific method." The scientific method is a standardized technique used in science and science education for investigating scientific or natural phenomena and deepening our understanding of how the world works. The scientific method usually follows a sequence like this:

1. Ask a question.
2. Do preliminary research on the question.
3. Construct a hypothesis, which is a possible explanation as to how or why something occurs.
4. Conduct an experiment or make intentional observations that test the hypothesis or try to show it is wrong.
5. Analyze the data and draw a conclusion.
6. Communicate the results by presenting your findings to others.

The scientific method can be useful for structuring a class investigation or for project-based learning. Perhaps some children in the class have noticed that the squirrels are eating the birdseed in the bird feeder in front of the school. This is a problem that will likely take some time and research to solve. Some content knowledge related to squirrels and birds will be important, in addition to some discussion regarding the actual design of the feeder.

We begin with a question: How can we stop the squirrels from eating the birdseed? As part of the scientific process, we can help the children conduct meaningful research. In this case, our research will likely involve watching the bird feeder and observing how the squirrels climb and move to reach the seeds. The children may record their observations by drawing pictures or dictating sentences to the teachers or a voice-to-text app.

Next, we invite children to create a hypothesis. A child may suggest, "The bird feeder is too low. The squirrels can climb it too easy." To test the hypothesis, the teacher hangs the bird feeder from a taller pole. The children observe again and test the hypothesis. Teachers facilitate this process by showing children the pictures they drew from their first observations: "Let's compare what happened before to what is happening now. What has changed?" This analysis might reveal that the taller pole has prevented the squirrels from reaching the birdseed.

Finally, an important part of the scientific process is sharing your results. The children can choose how to share their work and with whom to share it. Perhaps they will create a display for their families. Or perhaps they might choose to write a letter to the birds and let them know what steps they took to protect their food.

CONTENT KNOWLEDGE

We get better at solving problems as we get older. One reason is because we gain experience solving problems. You may have heard the old saying, "Experience is the best teacher." In the course of an ordinary day, we are exposed to a variety of situations at home, work, and school. We learn to close a window when we feel a draft. We learn to jiggle the handle when the toilet makes that funny noise. We use our direct experience to solve problems in practical ways. But another reason we get better at solving problems is because we gain knowledge about how things work, and that content knowledge informs our problem solving. Content knowledge is informed, academic, and often broader than practical experience.

When I began teaching young children, I didn't yet understand the importance of content knowledge in early childhood education. It wasn't talked about much in my graduate program. I don't think I even heard the term *content knowledge* until just a few years ago, which is just a fancy way of referring to the facts and concepts that are specific to a topic of study or subject area, such as science, math, language arts, or social studies. Early childhood teachers tend to be generalists because we usually don't receive much training in specific subject areas. So, for example, when I was teaching preschool and a child asked how a toilet works, I had neither the practical knowledge of plumbing nor the content knowledge about water systems to have anything to offer. At the time, I simply said, "What an interesting question!" I hadn't yet learned to guide an inquiry and provide opportunities for children to research and explore the answers to their provocative questions.

NAEYC's most recent revision of the Developmentally Appropriate Practice Position Statement includes offering content knowledge as a significant part of guiding children's play (NAEYC 2020). Early childhood educators are encouraged to consider our role in guiding play on a continuum between children's self-directed play and direct instruction. Somewhere between those ends of the continuum is a sweet spot where educators can use children's interests, questions, and problems to introduce new vocabulary and concepts across subject areas. As the problem-solving strategies presented throughout this book demonstrate, we can hit that sweet spot when we allow children to take the initial lead and point us toward a topic or idea worthy of our attention. Then teachers respond and facilitate, offering supports and, at times, some direct instruction that will guide children toward the solutions and new understandings.

A Developmentally Appropriate Research Process

When exploring topics of interest, researching specific questions, or solving problems, teachers can lead, model, and facilitate a research process that demonstrates to children how to find accurate information. Because most preschoolers are not yet readers and most academic sources are text-based, early childhood educators must be creative in finding information that is accessible to and understandable for young children.

An active, meaningful, and relevant research process with children may include seeking out people, places, and things.

- **People**—Is there anyone in your school community who is an expert on this topic? In the case of the question "How does a toilet work?" I could have looked for a parent or family member who is a plumber or has some other experience with plumbing.

- **Places**—Is there a place the children could visit (in person or virtually) where they could learn more about this topic? Perhaps the local home improvement store or nearby water filtration plant would allow the class to visit and ask questions of the staff.

- **Things**—What print and digital resources are available on this topic? Don't just google it! It's unlikely that a general search engine will readily give you information that is appropriate for young children. There are online reference tools specifically designed for children, such as Britannica Kids, PebbleGo, and DK Find Out! Consult with the children's librarian at your local public library. In the case of the plumbing question, a librarian could help you find nonfiction picture books about water systems and utilities, such as David Macaulay's brilliant *Toilet: How It Works*.

Play is essential for all children. As stated in the Developmentally Appropriate Practice Position Statement, "Play promotes joyful learning that fosters self-regulation, language, cognitive and social competencies as well as content knowledge across disciplines" (NAEYC 2020, 9). The problems that arise during play are as essential as the play itself. Like the yeast that makes the dough rise, problems grow new ideas and understandings. If there were no problems, the play would be flat, lacking the challenge that promotes learning. As educators, our job is to create the conditions in which the most interesting problems will arise and be solved within the context of active and joyful play.

CHAPTER 9

Measuring Growth

Throughout this book, I've advocated for an open-ended approach to solving problems. Most problems that occur in an early childhood classroom can be solved in more than one way. Yet I must acknowledge that in some situations, such as an addition or subtraction problem, most would agree that there exists a single "correct" solution. Sometimes our answers and solutions are wrong.

It's helpful to acknowledge the important role mistakes play in assessing children's growth and progress. Mistakes show us what we don't know. They are benchmarks that we can use to inform our teaching and learning. Mistakes are valuable information for children as well as teachers. As discussed in chapter 1, nurturing resilience and growth mindsets in children means drawing their attention to the way their minds work (metacognition) so they can become more aware of their own growth and progress.

For example, many preschool and kindergarten teachers begin a new school year by inviting children to draw self-portraits and write their names. This assessment activity tells the teachers a lot about each child's small-motor skills and early literacy skills. The activity deepens in value when teachers ask children to do the same thing on the last day of school. Usually the contrast is quite dramatic. Inviting children to compare their "before and after" work includes them in the assessment process and contributes to the development of a growth mindset. *Look how much we've learned!*

I don't advocate for standardized testing in the early years, but it is certainly possible to collect quantitative data about children's growth and progress in developmentally appropriate ways. In many preschool and kindergarten classrooms, teachers track the number of letters, numbers, and shapes that children can identify, and they record that data using checklists or assessment apps. This information is routinely shared with parents and guardians at family-teacher conferences or through digital communication systems. Some of this information can even be shared with the children themselves, as long as it is presented as a celebration of growth, rather than a stern directive to do better.

Is It Okay to Correct Children?

> If a child gives a wrong answer, I don't want to shut them down. I might say, "Okay, tell me what you think about that?" I allow wait time. I don't correct them. I might come back to the topic again another time.
>
> —S.G., pre-K teacher in Chicago, Illinois

At the time of this writing, there are high-profile discussions in the media about the teaching of mathematics. Educators seeking to dismantle racism in math instruction are challenging the ways we teach children to value accuracy. They suggest that a rigid drive to arrive at a single correct answer could be a factor in the underperformance of students of color in mathematics (Anderson 2017; Nierenberg 2021).

What relevance, if any, does this issue carry in early childhood education? I don't have an answer yet, but the debate affirms something early childhood educators have known for a long time—that process matters more than product. How we arrive at an answer is more important than the answer itself. The value of engaging children in a creative, collaborative process is the unifying thread throughout this book.

Suppose a preschool teacher is teaching a group lesson on shapes. The teacher holds up a picture card showing a full moon and asks, "What is the shape of the moon?" A child answers, "A triangle!" The child has given a wrong answer. But why? What's going on here, and how should you respond?

Here are some suggestions for responding to a child's wrong answer:

TAKE YOUR TIME

Giving children time to think was one of the most frequent suggestions from the teachers I interviewed for this book. Not just time to think in the moment but also time to go away and come back to a problem with a fresh perspective. In the case of the child who answered, "A triangle!" the teacher can pause and wait a moment before responding. Perhaps the child misspoke and meant to say "circle"?

INVITE CHILDREN TO EXPLAIN THEIR THINKING

Asking a follow-up question, such as "Tell me what you're thinking. Why do you think the moon is a triangle?" Remember that young children are still learning how to talk about what's going on inside their heads. They may not be able to articulate how they arrived at an answer. Teachers can scaffold this process for children by asking additional questions, such as, "Tell me what you know about triangles. Can you point to a triangle somewhere in this room?"

INDIVIDUALIZE YOUR APPROACH

Some children are more vulnerable than others when it comes to having someone correct their mistakes. Tailor your approach according to what you know about each child's personality, temperament, and skill level. Children who have experienced abuse or trauma may be particularly fearful of making mistakes.

Value Mistakes

As discussed in chapter 3, teachers in a mistake-friendly classroom set the stage for welcoming mistakes and problems at the beginning of the year and serve as role models who frequently acknowledge their own mistakes. The language of the classroom community includes phrases and expressions such as "Everyone makes mistakes" and "Let's figure it out!"

Additionally, you can add selections from the following list of children's books about mistakes and problems to your classroom library and share them at times when children need reminders that mistakes help us learn and grow.

A Bargain for Frances by Russell Hoban

Beautiful Oops! by Barney Saltzberg

The Book of Mistakes by Corinna Luyken

Crazy Hair Day by Barney Saltzberg

The Day Roy Riegels Ran the Wrong Way by Dan Gutman

Eraser by Anna Kang

Even Superheroes Make Mistakes by Shelly Becker

The Girl and the Bicycle by Mark Pett

The Girl Who Never Made Mistakes by Mark Pett and Gary Rubinstein

Giraffes Can't Dance by Giles Andreae

I Am a Thief by Abigail Rayner

Ish by Peter H. Reynolds

It's Okay to Make Mistakes by Todd Parr

The Lumberjack's Beard by Duncan Beedie

Mary Had a Little Lab by Sue Fliess

The Mixed-Up Truck by Stephen Savage

The Most Magnificent Thing by Ashley Spires

The Octopuppy by Martin McKenna

One by Kathryn Otoshi

Only One You by Linda Kranz

A Pair of Red Clogs by Masako Matsuno

Rosie Revere, Engineer by Andrea Beaty

Zero by Kathryn Otoshi

Documenting the Problem-Solving Process

Documentation is essential in assessing children's growth and development. Focusing our documentation efforts on the ongoing problem-solving processes that occur in the classroom provides a rich variety of evidence of learning.

Educators who follow the Reggio approach often use the phrase "making learning visible" to apply both to the children's own representations of their ideas, such as drawings or clay models, as well as to the teacher's research, which includes the documentation that teachers collect over time, such as notes and photos.

Reggio-inspired educator Pam Oken-Wright (2001) describes the documentation of learning as "both mirror and light" for the whole learning community—teachers, children, and families. She states, "We see ourselves, our thinking, and our process reflected as we live the process of documentation. Unlike a mirror's reflection, however, which is temporal—gone as soon as we step away from the mirror—documentation leaves the image reflected behind for as long as we'll have it, lighting our way along the path of negotiated learning" (15).

Documentation of a single problem-solving process can be collected in a digital or hard copy portfolio. Contents of a portfolio may include the following:

TEXT

- teacher notes
- teacher reflections

- quotations or transcripts from children's conversations
- dictated responses from children

SAMPLES OR IMAGES OF CHILDREN'S WORK

- drawings
- sketches
- maps
- diagrams
- writing

DIGITAL DOCUMENTATION

- video recordings
- audio recordings
- photos

For example, a portfolio documenting the problem of the flooded sandbox mentioned in chapter 5 might include a photo of the big puddle at the time of the discovery, quotations from the children documenting their initial responses to the problem, the list of possible solutions, photos of the children using an old towel to clean up the sandbox, and the drawings children made later as they reflected on what happened.

Tell the Story

The teacher's job is to organize the documentation into some kind of useful whole: to make meaning of a collection of pieces of documentation, think of the problem-solving process as a story, and organize the documentation in a way that tells the tale.

As humans, so many of our favorite stories are about big problems that characters struggle to overcome. Some writers and psychologists argue that every story follows pretty much the same structure. Literature professor Joseph Campbell identified one of the most iconic story structures as "the hero's journey." In short, a hero's journey includes a call to action, such as heading off on a trip, followed by a trial or challenge of some kind, and then, finally, a battle or struggle that results in an ultimate victory or growth. For example, take Simba, the main character in the popular film and musical *The Lion King*. The problem Simba must solve is epic: he must save the entire lion kingdom from his evil uncle, Scar. (Spoiler alert—Simba succeeds!) What a snooze the story would have been if Simba didn't have any problems to solve.

Your documentation and portfolios are representations of the problems that make us think and make us human. The children in your class are the heroes of their own journeys. Tell their stories.

CHAPTER 10

Celebrating Problems

The problems we solve with young children are too good to keep inside our classrooms. We must share them with others! And the people most interested in the children's progress are their parents and family members.

Engaging in reciprocal partnerships with families is an essential task for early childhood educators. The importance of building trust with families, especially with parents and primary caregivers, is emphasized in the NAEYC (2020) position statement on developmentally appropriate practice. How we share news about the problems we solve and how we celebrate children's abilities to solve those problems can play an important role in building trusting relationships. We can also provide supports and resources to families that will help them nurture problem-solving skills at home.

Connecting with Parents

Parents may be some of the most vulnerable people you will meet. Our society judges parents harshly every day. Glaring evidence of this can be found in social media as well as in public policy. At the same time, parents are driven by an intense desire to protect and care for their young children. It's no wonder it can be difficult for parents to talk about their children's problems and mistakes.

Let's look at some specific strategies for incorporating problem solving into parent communication and collaboration with families.

SET THE STAGE

As described in chapter 3, set the stage for a mistake-friendly classroom at the start of the school year as part of your orientation for families and caregivers. Let them know the problems that arise in the classroom will be used as teachable moments and opportunities for meaningful learning. Families will know you mean what you say if you show your own vulnerability and demonstrate your own grace under pressure when you make mistakes yourself. Show the families that you are willing to apologize and take responsibility when things go wrong, and they will begin to trust you.

COMMUNICATE

As you regularly communicate with families about the events and happenings in the classroom, share stories and documentation that demonstrate how you use problems as opportunities for growth and learning. Share articles and resources about what it means to have a growth mindset.

BUILD RELATIONSHIPS

Building reciprocal partnerships with families takes time and intention. NAEYC's 2020 revision to the Developmentally Appropriate Practice Position Statement emphasizes the importance of considering the child's context within their family—including the family's culture, language, values, and socioeconomic status. Recommendations include maintaining frequent two-way communication, providing multiple opportunities for family participation, respecting each family's choices and preferences, and learning about the community. I would also add demonstrating patience, empathy, and humor around mistakes and problems as an important element in building partnerships with families.

CREATE COMMUNITY

Include families in documenting and celebrating problems and mistakes by inviting their participation and input. At class gatherings and school events, invite families to tell stories about funny family mishaps and surprises. Throw a party for families to celebrate all the wonderful problems the children have solved.

Notice How Families Solve Problems

To help families support children's problem solving at home, it's important to gain some understanding of how parents and other family members approach problems. Family culture, economic status, and prior life experience are just a few factors that may influence how family members feel and act when they encounter a challenge.

For example, you may observe a parent at the end of the school day discovering that the zipper on their child's coat is broken and won't close. How does the parent respond? A parent with a strong sense of humor may crack a joke about the "extra ventilation" the jacket now provides. A stressed and exhausted parent may respond with anger and scold the child for not taking better care with the jacket. An especially affectionate parent may respond with tender care for the child, tucking the sides of the jacket together and snuggling the child in their arms. Another parent may respond with patient determination, fiddling with the zipper to try to fix the alignment. These observations can tell you a lot about how the parent and the family respond to problems and challenges.

Informal, friendly conversations with parents and family members can also build your understanding of how a child's family approaches problems. An open-ended question such as "How was your day today?" might turn into a discussion of how the parent solved a problem or responded to a challenge at work or home. Maybe a mom who works as a server in a restaurant mentions with frustration that the kitchen was short staffed and her orders were delayed. We might affirm this parent's challenging day in the same way we support children who are experiencing struggles by acknowledging their emotions and asking more questions: "How frustrating! What did you do? How did you manage?" The parent will likely appreciate the opportunity to vent, and you may discover that this parent is resourceful and resilient in their approach to problems: "It was hard, but I just kept smiling and refilling everyone's coffee and water until the food was ready."

Families under stress, especially those experiencing significant economic, emotional, or medical challenges, may be less flexible, optimistic, and resilient when it comes to solving problems. It's important to recognize the significant toll these challenges can take on families. At the same time, look for sources of strength—in a shared faith, perhaps, or in connections to an extended family or community. Look for individual strengths in parents and family members, such as humor, patience, grace, and ingenuity.

Help Families Solve Problems at Home

I have a vivid childhood memory of a day I helped my family solve a problem. My mother, my brothers, and I were on our way to the grocery store on a snowy day. My mother was driving our family station wagon and we were stopped at an intersection when a large tree limb, heavy with snow, fell with a big thud on the roof of the car. We all got out to look. The car was not damaged in any obvious way, but branches and leaves covered the windshield, and the limb was too heavy to push off the roof of the car. My mother wasn't sure what to do. This was in the age before cell phones, and it would have been difficult to walk to a gas station or garage to get help. I noticed that the branch was still attached to the tree, and I asked my mother, "What if we just try driving away? Maybe the branch will just stay stuck on the tree." My mother agreed to try. We all got back in the car, and my mother slowly inched the car forward. Sure enough, the connection between the branch and the tree held, and we extricated the car from the limb. I'll never forget the praise I received for solving that problem for my family. I think that incident played a big role in my developing a sense of confidence around solving problems.

As early childhood educators, we can make suggestions and offer resources that will help families empower their children to develop problem-solving skills and nurture their children's sense of confidence and resilience. Here are five ways to begin.

ENCOURAGE A SHIFT FROM PUNISHMENT TO PROBLEM SOLVING

When children make mistakes or do something wrong at home, adults often respond with discipline. For example, at dinner, if a child accidentally drops and breaks a dish, the parent may scold, "You must be more careful," and punish the child by making them leave the table or sit in a corner. This approach is common, but by removing the child from the situation they caused, we lose the opportunity to teach the child how to engage in an active problem-solving process.

We can help families shift their thinking from punishment to problem solving. As educators, we have many opportunities to share information with families about how to discipline or set limits with children. We can talk about these issues at family meetings and share resources in newsletters and on bulletin boards, both in print and online.

For example, we can help families understand that when a child breaks a dish at the dinner table, this is an opportunity for the child to learn to take responsibility for what happened by helping to solve the problems they created. Truly, there are many wonderful problems to solve here. First, there is the immediate problem of the broken dish. How will we clean this up? Then there is the problem of repairing or replacing what has been lost. If food has been spilled, how will we make sure everyone has enough to eat? And can the dish be repaired? And finally, there is the broader problem of how to prevent this from happening again.

Even very young children can be part of the process and take an active role in creating solutions to these problems. A child may be too young to safely clean up the shards of a broken dish, but perhaps they could help hold the bag used to collect the pieces. If some food has been lost in the process, the child can be offered a choice: "Your biscuit fell on the floor, and it can't be eaten now. Would you rather have a cracker or a piece of bread?" Later, after everyone has recovered a bit from the drama of the moment, a parent can have a heart-to-heart talk with the child about how to prevent this type of spill from happening again. Perhaps the child already knows what to do: "Next time, I need to make sure I don't put my dishes near the edge of the table."

Discussing these kinds of scenarios with parents and caregivers at family meetings or in more informal settings can help parents look for opportunities to choose problem solving over punishment.

ASK GREAT QUESTIONS

Many of the prompts and questions offered in chapter 4 are as useful and effective at home as they are in the classroom. Offer families a few suggestions for starting a problem-solving conversation with their child, such as "Let's talk about what's going on" or "I'm ready to help you solve this problem."

Create a handout for families listing a few questions they can ask their children when families encounter mistakes, problems, accidents, and challenges. These may include some of our "greatest hits" from chapter 4:

- What do you see?
- What are you thinking?
- What are some ways we might solve this problem?
- What idea should we try first?
- If this problem happens again, what would you do?

Talk about how and when to use these questions at family meetings, in family-teacher conferences, and in ordinary informal conversations with families. When parents are present in the classroom, model how to ask children these questions. Try choosing and promoting a "Question of the Month" to post and practice at school and at home.

ASSIGN SMALL PROBLEMS TO SOLVE AT HOME

Some families do not have a lot of knowledge of child development and may need your help determining which kinds of problems are appropriate for a young child to solve. Create a list of small problems, challenges, or tasks that families can intentionally offer their children at home. This list might include the following:

- Wiping up a spill
- Putting dirty spoons in the dishwasher
- Placing cardboard boxes inside each other to fit in a recycling bin
- Organizing clothes in a drawer
- Matching the right size lid for a plastic food-storage container
- Searching for something that is lost or missing (keys, cell phone, dog's leash, and so on)

Young children may not have the patience and stamina to complete all these tasks on their own, but let families know that the simple act of inviting children to participate in these processes will empower them to take a more active role in family problem solving as they grow older.

MAKE PROBLEM SOLVING A GAME

As children grow older, families can nurture children's creative thinking by inviting them to consider more than one way to solve a problem. This process could be turned into a family game called Try Another Way or Think of Three. Suppose a parent and child are playing catch outdoors and their ball gets stuck on the roof of their garage. A first attempt to poke the ball with a stick fails to dislodge the ball. The parent can embrace the problem-solving challenge by saying, "It's time to play Try Another Way. Let's think of a new way to solve this problem." Similarly, a child could be challenged even further by Think of Three, a game that requires brainstorming at least three solutions. Some ideas might be silly and impractical, such as "Let's grow some wings and fly up to the roof," but the gamification of the problem-solving process encourages creative thinking and new ideas.

OFFER AFFIRMATIONS

Sometimes families are so busy and overwhelmed they just want us, the experts, to tell them what to say to their children. Here, offer families affirming statements that will communicate trust and confidence to their children. These might include such statements as the following:

- "You are my problem-solver."
- "I like the way you solve problems."
- "You have so many good ideas."
- "You are learning how to solve problems."

Print a few affirmations on a card and give these cards to families to keep in their pockets or to take home and post on their refrigerators. If the families in your program speak languages other than English, have the affirmations translated into their home languages. While not everyone is open to practicing affirmations, many adults and children respond with enthusiasm. Overall, be patient and understand that for many families, welcoming problems and embracing mistakes is a very new and unfamiliar approach. Each small step is valuable progress.

Key Takeaways

I offer three key takeaways that summarize this book.

Problems are everywhere.

The problems will come whether or not you welcome them. Why not make the most of them? The problems that arise from the children's direct experiences will be more engaging and meaningful to the children than any lesson plan or curriculum book.

Children are capable.

Don't be afraid to let children take the lead. Usually children are much more capable than we expect.

We are role models.

The children are always watching us to see how we respond to surprises and difficulties. If we want to teach children to respond to problems with excitement, curiosity, patience, and grace, we must also be willing to cultivate those qualities in ourselves.

The Hard Truth

Not every problem has a solution, at least not immediately. This is an important but difficult lesson to learn, for adults as well as children. Sometimes our job is to help children determine what they have control over and what they do not and to make the best of whatever limited resources are available.

If you and the children are struggling to solve a problem, be ready to take more time another day. Leave it alone and come back to the problem later. Say to the children, "It looks like we don't have everything we need to solve this problem" or "Let's hold on to these ideas for later." When we must leave a problem unresolved, we can still acknowledge feelings and support one another: "Let's do everything we can to help our friends feel better until we can solve this problem."

The hard truth is that some problems can't be solved. Some losses must be grieved. One of our jobs as teachers is to show children how to sit with the discomfort of not knowing all the answers.

Some problems are so big and so deep, they will take years to solve. Some take a whole lifetime. Some longer. There is the saying, "Blessed are those who plant trees knowing they will not live to sit in the shade of their foliage." We can strive to remain open to the possibility of new answers becoming visible in the future.

In the end, we are a community of lifelong learners. It is the striving for connection and understanding that makes us human and gives us purpose.

References

Anderson, Melinda D. 2017. "How Does Race Affect a Student's Math Education?" *Atlantic*, April 25. www.theatlantic.com/education/archive/2017/04/racist-math-education/524199.

ASHA (American-Speech-Language-Hearing Association). 2022. "How Does Your Child Hear and Talk?" Accessed February 10. www.asha.org/public/speech/development/chart.

Biermeier, Mary Ann. 2015. "Inspired by Reggio Emilia: Emergent Curriculum in Relationship-Driven Learning Environments." *Young Children* 70 (5). www.naeyc.org/resources/pubs/yc/nov2015/emergent-curriculum.

Blank, Jolyn, and Stefanie Lynch. 2018. "Growing in STEM. The Design Process: Engineering Practices in Preschool." *Young Children* 73 (4). www.naeyc.org/resources/pubs/yc/sep2018/design-process-engineering-preschool.

Boaler, Jo. 2016. *Mathematical Mindsets: Unleashing Students' Potential through Creative Math, Inspiring Messages, and Innovative Teaching*. San Francisco, CA: Jossey-Bass.

Boston Children's Museum. 2016. "'The Land': A Movie and Discussion about Adventure Play, Part 1." Streamed live October 5. YouTube video, 19:24. www.youtube.com/watch?v=vHKrH51ygok.

Carter, Margie, and Deb Curtis. 1994. *Training Teachers: A Harvest of Theory and Practice*. St. Paul, MN: Redleaf Press.

CASEL (Collaborative for Academic, Social, and Emotional Learning). 2022. "CASEL'S SEL Framework: What Are the Core Competence Areas and Where Are They Promoted?" Accessed March 7. https://casel.org/casel-sel-framework-11-2020.

Center on the Developing Child at Harvard University. 2007. "InBrief: The Science of Early Childhood Development." https://developingchild.harvard.edu/resources/inbrief-science-of-ecd.

Curtis, Deb, and Nadia Jaboneta. 2019. *Children's Lively Minds: Schema Theory Made Visible*. St. Paul, MN: Redleaf Press.

Derman-Sparks, Louise, and Julie Olsen Edwards. 2020. *Anti-Bias Education for Young Children and Ourselves.* 2nd ed. With Catherine Goins. Washington, DC: National Association for the Education of Young Children.

Dewey, John. 1910. *How We Think.* Boston: Heath & Co.

Dombro, Amy L., Judy Jablon, and Charlotte Stetson. 2020. *Powerful Interactions: How to Connect with Children to Extend Their Learning.* 2nd ed. Washington, DC: National Association for the Education of Young Children.

Duckworth, Angela. 2016. *Grit: The Power of Passion and Perseverance.* New York: Scribner.

Dweck, Carol S. 2007. "Is Math a Gift? Beliefs That Put Females at Risk." In *Why Aren't More Women in Science? Top Researchers Debate the Evidence,* edited by Stephen J. Ceci and Wendy M. Williams, 47–55. Washington, DC: American Psychological Association. https://doi.org/10.1037/11546-004.

Evans, Betsy. 2009. *You're Not My Friend Anymore! Illustrated Answers to Questions about Young Children's Challenging Behaviors.* Ypsilanti, MI: HighScope.

Friedman, Susan, and Alissa Mwenelupembe, eds. 2020. *Each and Every Child: Teaching Preschool with an Equity Lens.* Washington, DC: National Association for the Education of Young Children.

Galinsky, Ellen. 2019. "From Trauma-Informed to Asset-Informed Care in Early Childhood." *Education Plus Development* (blog), Brookings Institution. October 23. www.brookings.edu/blog/education-plus-development/2019/10/23/from-trauma-informed-to-asset-informed-care-in-early-childhood.

Hannon, Claudina. 2022. "Reinforcing Language Skills for Our Youngest Learners." National Association for the Education of Young Children. Accessed February 10. www.naeyc.org/our-work/families/reinforcing-language-skills.

Hansel, Rosanne Regan. 2021. *Exploring the 3-D World: Developing Spatial and Math Skills in Young Children.* St. Paul, MN: Redleaf Press.

Harris, Nadine Burke. 2018. *The Deepest Well: Healing the Long-Term Effects of Childhood Adversity.* Boston: Mariner Books.

Henningsen, Marjorie. 2013. "Making Sense of Experience in Preschool: Children's Encounters with Numeracy and Literacy through Inquiry." *South African Journal of Childhood Education* 3 (2): 41–55. https://files.eric.ed.gov/fulltext/EJ1187263.pdf.

Iruka, Iheoma U., Stephanie M. Curenton, Tonia R. Durden, and Kerry-Ann Escayg. 2020. *Don't Look Away: Embracing Anti-Bias Classrooms.* Lewisville, NC: Gryphon House.

Lindfors, Judith Wells. 1999. *Children's Inquiry: Using Language to Make Sense of the World.* New York: Teachers College Press.

MacLaughlin, Sarah S. 2022. "Helping Young Children with Sharing." Zero to Three. Accessed February 10. www.zerotothree.org/resources/1964-helping-young-children-with-sharing.

Malaguzzi, Loris. 2022. "100 Languages." Translated by Lella Gandini. Accessed February 14. Reggio Children. www.reggiochildren.it/en/reggio-emilia-approach/100-linguaggi-en.

Moser, Jason S., et al. 2011. "Mind Your Errors: Evidence for a Neural Mechanism Linking Growth Mind-Set to Adaptive Posterror Adjustments." *Psychological Science* 22: 1484. https://doi.org/10.1177/0956797611419520.

NAEYC (National Association for the Education of Young Children). 2020. "Developmentally Appropriate Practice (DAP) Position Statement." www.naeyc.org/resources/position-statements/dap/contents.

National Research Council. 2000. *Inquiry and the National Science Education Standards: A Guide for Teaching and Learning.* Washington, DC: National Academies Press. https://doi.org/10.17226/9596.

Nierenberg, Amelia. 2021. "Should California De-Track Math?" *New York Times*, November 10. www.nytimes.com/2021/11/10/us/california-math-curriculum.html.

Oken-Wright, Pam. 2001. "Documentation: Both Mirror and Light." *Innovations in Early Education: The International Reggio Exchange* 8 (4): 5–15. www.reggioalliance.org/downloads/documentation:okenwright.pdf.

Owens, Melinda T., and Kimberly D. Tanner. 2017. "Teaching as Brain Changing: Exploring Connections between Neuroscience and Innovative Teaching". *CBE Life Sci Educ.* 2017 Summer; 16 (2): fe2. www.ncbi.nlm.nih.gov/pmc/articles/PMC5459260.

Paley, Vivian Gussin. 1981. *Wally's Stories: Conversations in the Kindergarten.* Cambridge, MA: Harvard University Press.

———. 1993. *You Can't Say You Can't Play.* Cambridge, MA: Harvard University Press.

———. 2004. *A Child's Work: The Importance of Fantasy Play.* Chicago: University of Chicago Press.

Pelo, Ann. 2014. "Find the Questions Worth Asking." *Child Care Exchange*, January/February, 50–53.

Pierce, Jan, and Cheryl Lynn Johnson. 2010. "Problem Solving with Young Children Using Persona Dolls." *Young Children* 65 (6): 106–8. https://eric.ed.gov/?id=EJ930001.

Sandseter, Ellen Beate Hansen, and Leif Edward Ottesen Kennair. 2011. "Children's Risky Play from an Evolutionary Perspective: The Anti-Phobic Effects of Thrilling Experiences." *Evolutionary Psychology* 9 (2): 257–84. https://journals.sagepub.com/doi/pdf/10.1177/147470491100900212.

Strasser, Janis, and Lisa Mufson Bresson. 2017. *Big Questions for Young Minds: Extending Children's Thinking.* Washington, DC: National Association for the Education of Young Children.

Tough, Paul. 2012. *How Children Succeed: Grit, Curiosity, and the Hidden Power of Character.* Boston: Houghton Mifflin Harcourt.

WIDA (World-Class Instructional Design and Assessment Consortium). 2020. *WIDA Early Years Guiding Principles of Language Development.* Madison: Board of Regents of the University of Wisconsin System. https://wida.wisc.edu/sites/default/files/resource/Guiding-Principles-of-Early-ELD.pdf.

Additional Resources

CHAPTER 1

Carol Dweck

www.ted.com/talks/carol_dweck_the_power_of_believing_that_you_can_improve

https://sparq.stanford.edu/solutions/growth-mindset-helps-girls-learn-math

Dweck, Carol. 2007. *Mindset: The New Psychology of Success.* New York: Ballantine Books.

Nadine Burke Harris

www.npr.org/sections/health-shots/2019/07/02/733896346/californias-first-surgeon-general-spotlights-health-risks-of-childhood-adversity

Harris, Nadine Burke. 2018. *The Deepest Well: Healing the Long-Term Effects of Childhood Adversity.* Mariner Books.

Paul Tough

www.theatlantic.com/magazine/archive/2016/06/how-kids-really-succeed/480744

Tough, Paul. 2012. *How Children Succeed: Grit, Curiosity, and the Hidden Power of Character.* Boston: Houghton Mifflin Harcourt.

CHAPTER 2

Carol Garhart Mooney

Mooney, Carol Garhart. 2013. *Theories of Childhood: An Introduction to Dewey, Montessori, Erikson, Piaget, and Vygotsky.* 2nd ed. St. Paul, MN: Redleaf Press.

Design Thinking

www.edsurge.com/news/2019-07-31-design-thinking-is-a-challenge-to-teach-and-that-s-a-good-thing

Inquiry-Based Learning

www.edutopia.org/article/embracing-inquiry-based-instruction

https://nau.pure.elsevier.com/en/publications/what-is-inquiry-based-learning

CHAPTER 3

Amy L. Dombro, Judy Jablon, and Charlotte Stetson

Dombro, Amy L., Judy Jablon, and Charlotte Stetson. 2020. *Powerful Interactions: How to Connect with Children to Extend Their Learning*. 2nd ed. Washington, DC: National Association for the Education of Young Children.

Vivian Gussin Paley

Paley, Vivian Gussin. 1981. *Wally's Stories: Conversations in the Kindergarten*. Cambridge, MA: Harvard University Press.

Design Engineering

www.eie.org/overview/engineering-design-process

https://asana.com/resources/iterative-process

CHAPTER 4

Ann Pelo

Pelo, Ann. 2014. "Find the Questions Worth Asking." *Child Care Exchange*, January/February, 50–53.

Steffen Saifer

Saifer, Steffen. 2018. *HOT Skills: Developing Higher-Order Thinking in Young Learners*. St. Paul, MN: Redleaf Press.

Sportscasting

www.janetlansbury.com/2013/04/5-benefits-of-sportscasting-your-childs-struggles

CHAPTER 5

Deb Curtis and Margie Carter

Curtis, Deb, and Margie Carter. 2011. *Reflecting Children's Lives: A Handbook for Planning Child-Centered Curriculum*. 2nd ed. St. Paul, MN: Redleaf Press.

Carolyn Edwards, Lella Gandini, and George Foreman

Edwards, Carolyn, Lella Gandini, and George Foreman, eds. 2011. *The Hundred Languages of Children: The Reggio Emilia Experience in Transformation*. 3rd ed. Westport, CT: Praeger.

Susan Stacey

Stacey, Susan. 2018. *Emergent Curriculum in Early Childhood Setting*. 2nd ed. St. Paul, MN: Redleaf Press.

CHAPTER 6

Helping Children Play and Learn Together
www.naeyc.org/files/yc/file/201001/OstroskyWeb0110.pdf

Vivian Gussin Paley
Paley, Vivian Gussin. 1993. *You Can't Say You Can't Play.* Cambridge, MA: Harvard University Press.

Buddy Benches
www.bbc.com/news/stories-45958313

CHAPTER 7

Carolyn Edwards, Lella Gandini, and George Foreman
Edwards, Carolyn, Lella Gandini, and George Foreman, eds. 2011. *The Hundred Languages of Children: The Reggio Emilia Experience in Transformation.* 3rd ed. Westport, CT: Praeger.

Typical Speech and Language Development
www.asha.org/public/speech/development

Supporting Dual-Language Learners
www.naeyc.org/resources/pubs/books/essentials-supporting-DLLs

Total Communication
www.sense.org.uk/get-support/information-and-advice/communication/total-communication

CHAPTER 8

Ann Gadzikowski
Gadzikowski, Ann. 2013. *Challenging Exceptionally Bright Children in Early Childhood Classrooms.* St. Paul, MN: Redleaf Press.

———. 2015. *Creating a Beautiful Mess: Ten Essential Play Experiences for a Joyous Childhood.* St. Paul, MN: Redleaf Press.

Vivian Gussin Paley
Paley, Vivian Gussin. 2004. *A Child's Work: The Importance of Fantasy Play.* Chicago: University of Chicago Press.

Playgrounds and Risky Play
www.theatlantic.com/magazine/archive/2014/04/hey-parents-leave-those-kids-alone/358631

CHAPTER 9

Judy Harris Helm, Sallee Beneke, and Kathy Steinheimer

Helm, Judy Harris, Sallee Beneke, and Kathy Steinheimer. 2007. *Windows on Learning: Documenting Young Children's Work*. 2nd ed. New York: Teachers College Press.

Racism in Math Education

www.the74million.org/article/can-right-answers-be-wrong-latest-clash-over-white-supremacy-culture-unfolds-in-unlikely-arena-math-class

Documentation

www.naeyc.org/sites/default/files/globally-shared/downloads/PDFs/resources/pubs/seitz.pdf

CHAPTER 10

Janis Keyser

Keyser, Janis. 2006. *From Parents to Partners: Building a Family-Centered Early Childhood Program*. St. Paul, MN: Redleaf Press; Washington, DC: National Association for the Education of Young Children.

Derry Koralek, Karen Nemeth, and Kelly Ramsey

Koralek, Derry, Karen Nemeth, and Kelly Ramsey. 2019. *Families and Educators Together: Building Great Relationships That Support Young Children*. Washington, DC: National Association for the Education of Young Children.

Mary Muhs

Muhs, Mary. 2018. *Family Engagement in Early Childhood Settings*. St. Paul, MN: Redleaf Press.

Index